The We
Organized
Camper

DATE DUE

The Well-Organized Camper

Linda Frederick Yaffe

CHICAGO
REVIEW
PRESS

Library of Congress Cataloging-in-Publication Data
Yaffe, Linda Frederick.
    The well-organized camper / Linda Frederick Yaffe ; [all
illustrations by Linda Frederick Yaffe]. — 1st ed.
        p.   cm.
    Includes bibliographical references and index.
    ISBN 1–55652–343–2
    1. Camping—Planning.   I. Title.
GV191.7.Y32   1999
796.54—dc21   98–51291
                                                                    CIP

Interior illustrations: Linda Frederick Yaffe

Published by Chicago Review Press, Incorporated
814 North Franklin Street
Chicago, Illinois 60610
ISBN 1-55652-343-2
Printed in the United States of America
5 4 3 2 1

With thanks to Lisa Rosenthal, my editor at Chicago Review Press.

"There is more danger that a man take too much than too little into the wilderness."

—Stewart Edward White, *Camp and Trail*, 1913

CONTENTS

INTRODUCTION

We fell asleep while camped on a quiet, empty beach. In the morning we woke to fog and large moving shapes. We sat up, startled, in our sleeping bags. The shapes came into our sleepy focus through the mist: a herd of elk. Roosevelt elk roamed the beach all around us; some waded into the shallow waves, others grazed in the sand dunes. The bull elk sensed our presence. He raised his antlered head, puffed his chest, and stepped toward us, shielding his cows and calves. The fog swirled around him. His coat glistened and his nostrils flared. Satisfied that we were not a threat, he and his herd resumed their quiet grazing.

* * *

Camping is thrilling, adventurous, inexpensive, and available to everyone. Wildlife, celestial shows, closeness with family and friends away from everyday distractions, all renew one's spirit.

Since it's so much fun, why doesn't everyone camp more frequently? We all suffer from inertia. If our camping equipment is in need of repair or replacement, if it lies scattered around the house, or if we aren't sure we have the necessary gear, we are not motivated to camp. *The Well-Organized Camper* will help you eliminate all the obstacles that get in the way of outdoor fun. Read Chapter 1, Plan to Have Fun, for an overview on how you can prepare at home for living comfortably outdoors. The basics listed in Chapter 1 apply to all types of camping, while later chapters offer specifics for specialized adventures. The hints in Chapter 2, Backpack in Comfort, will interest all campers who walk, paddle, or ski away from their vehicles for one or more nights.

> ### Less Is More
>
> **Use the information in this book to plan and organize your camping trips. A well-organized camper spends less time working and more time having fun. There are a few secrets for frequent, pleasurable camping trips.**

What type of camping suits you? My brother, a sedentary gourmet chef, would never join me backpacking in the remote high country. He prefers car camping, not too far from New York City. His camping equipment includes a gigantic tent, a cot, and a large library of books. You can camp simply, with few pieces of equipment, or luxuriously, with a lot of gear. You can live outdoors inexpensively using pots and pans and a blanket roll from home, or you can buy the latest lightweight, high-tech equipment. The choice is yours.

Perhaps you are new to camping and want to try a short backpack trip, an overnight paddling trip, a winter-camping vacation, or a camping adventure with your children. Maybe you'd like to try camping, instead of staying in hotels, during your next trip abroad. This book will show you how to get organized for all of these adventures. If you are an experienced camper, the tips in this book will make your trips safer, more comfortable, and much more fun.

We all make mistakes while learning to live away from home's amenities. You will likely experience a certain camping error only one time, then learn from your mistake, and never repeat it. Your mistakes will live on only as humorous anecdotes. Even better, learn from my mistakes, and the mistakes of others, described in this book. The more you learn and experience, the simpler camping becomes.

I've always loved to camp. As a youngster, I believed that camping was special but separate—not part of real life. Now in my 50s, after more than 40 years of wonderful camping adventures, I know that living outdoors *is* real life. It is a continuously running show that awaits you.

- *Simplify.* Plan to do less and see more. Cover less distance; don't rush.
- Use the *equipment lists* in this book for backpacking, car camping, camping with children, paddling trips, winter camping, and international camping. Take only the equipment you really need.
- Keep your gear *organized*, boxed, and ready to go. Get it together once, then keep it together.
- *Schedule* time for camping trips and go!

1

PLAN TO HAVE FUN

While running my first marathon, I realized that the race itself was simply one part of a larger process. The marathon began much earlier, while preparing physically and mentally. In the same way, your camping trip begins at home, not at the trailhead. Time spent preparing eliminates stress while you're on vacation. It also creates extra time for pleasure. When you have planned well, your outdoor adventure will be worry-free. The food and equipment you are carrying, the destination you've chosen, and the route you've selected to get there will determine the quality of your experience.

Do Less, See More

Your comfort, safety, and enjoyment will be greatly increased by scaling down your camping plans. Choose a realistic trip, one that suits your interests and abilities. Don't turn your vacation into drudgery by taking a trip that is too long or too difficult. A car camping trip is more fun if most of your time is spent relaxing at a shady campsite rather than sitting behind the wheel of your vehicle on the highway. A backpack trip will feel comfortable rather than exhausting if you plan to cover less distance and if you allow time for rest days at base camps.

> **A backpack trip will feel comfortable rather than exhausting if you plan to cover less distance and if you allow time for rest days at base camps.**

The fun part of camping is the time spent living outdoors. For most people, living outdoors means relaxing in camp, exploring near camp, and taking time to experience the beauty of the place. When you stop late in the day, you're tired. It's dark. Hiking, paddling a boat, or driving your vehicle from dawn to dusk isn't a vacation; it's work. Instead, plan to stop early. Enjoy the additional leisure hours around camp.

Allow extra hours and days when planning all of your trips. A week-long backpack route requiring 12 miles of steep, high altitude hiking every single day is too grueling for most campers. You would notice only the few feet of trail in front of you as you pushed to complete the circuit. Yes, you could do it, but would you want to? If you have two weeks to spend in Europe, don't try to camp in three different countries. You will experience virtually nothing; most of your time will be spent traveling between countries and adjusting to different cultures and languages. Cut back, way back, and greatly increase your pleasure.

Equipment Lists

"Dry and sunny this weekend . . ."

While driving home from work on Friday, you hear the weather forecast. The weekend will be perfect. You decide to go camping.

You can camp on short notice because you've organized ahead of time. No need to go shopping; you previously prepared a wide variety of home-dried one-pot meals. From your boxes of ready-to-pack gear, you quickly check off the items on your equipment list. In less than an hour you've changed your clothes and packed the equipment in the car. You're ready to go.

Use the lists in this book for backpacking, car camping, camping with children, paddling trips, winter camping, and international camping. What you take with you and what you leave behind will make or break your trip. Make it a habit: check off each item as you pack it. No matter how experienced you are, equipment lists are a basic necessity. Your tent is useless if you have left the tent poles at home in the closet. Equipment lists free you from the strain of trying to remember what you need and from wondering whether or not you've already packed it. When you have checked off each item on your equipment list as you packed it, your mind can be at ease. You know you are carrying exactly what you need—no more, no less. Equipment lists are virtually the same for a three-month trip or for a three-day trip; only the amount of food varies. Safety and comfort needs remain constant.

> **Equipment lists free you from the strain of trying to remember what you need and from wondering whether or not you've already packed it.**

Ready-to-Pack Equipment Boxes

Devote part of a closet to your equipment. Controlled room temperatures are best for storage of your gear. Avoid the extreme heat and cold of the attic, garage, or outside storeroom. Coated nylon and other treated fabrics and inflatable kayaks and rafts are especially sensitive to heat. Make room in a closet inside your house for your camping gear.

> **After each trip, examine your equipment before replacing it in the closet. If some pieces of gear need to be cleaned, repaired, or replaced, take care of them now.**

Protect your closet's flooring from pokes and scrapes from skis, ice axes, or walking sticks. Cover the floor with a clean old tarp, sheets of cardboard, or thick layers of newspaper. Inside the closet, store most of your equipment in boxes. Label one box for car camping, another for backpacking, and other boxes for the specialty trips you enjoy, such as ski touring or international travel. Use sturdy boxes that are similarly sized, so they stack easily. Covered plastic tubs or simply heavy, covered cardboard boxes will last for years. Tents and sleeping bags can be stored loosely folded on the closet's shelf or hung from the rod. Other large equipment can be hung, shelved, or stood upright in the corners of the closet.

After each trip, examine your equipment before replacing it in the closet. If some pieces of gear need to be cleaned, repaired, or replaced, take care of them now, during the next few days. Tents and sleeping bags are expensive and somewhat fragile; they especially need loving care. If you treat them gently, your tent and sleeping bag will stay in good condition for many years. Remove them from their stuff sacks. Sponge clean any dirt spots with a small amount of mild soap and warm water.

Wash your sleeping bag by hand only when absolutely necessary. Use a small amount of mild soap in warm water. Spot cleaning and airing will keep your bag clean

Store your sleeping bag loosely between trips.

in between infrequent washings. Let the tent and sleeping bag air dry, then store them loosely folded or hung.

Try to keep your sleeping bag as clean as possible. In camping situations where the weight of your equipment is not a consideration, such as a car camping trip or a float trip on a large raft, use a sleeping bag liner to keep the inside of your bag clean. Lightweight sheet-sacks made of nylon or silk are designed for hosteling or backpacking. Heavier sleeping bag liners are made of cotton, flannel, or fleece. Sheet-sacks and sleeping bag liners are available from camping and travel stores. A basic liner is easily sewn by folding a cotton, nylon, or flannel sheet in half, lengthwise, and stitching a seam along the bottom and the side.

Equipment Adjustment

Get used to walking while wearing your boots and carrying your full-sized backpack or smaller daypack. As you plan your camping trip, reacquaint yourself with walking and being outdoors and assess your equipment at the same time. Walk instead of driving. Walk to work or walk every day during your lunch hour. Shop for groceries while wearing your pack and hiking boots. Feel how your pack rides when it is loaded. Adjust your pack: shorten or lengthen the shoulder straps, sew or tape extra padding around the waist belt or the shoulder straps, if needed. Add a sternum strap for better weight distribution.

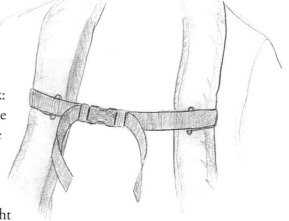

sternum strap

Even if you have been wearing the same pack for years, keep evaluating its fit. Your posture and figure change and packs shift and stretch. Create instant padding over your hipbones. Tie a jacket or sweater around your hips; wear it underneath the pack's waist belt.

Bag It

Whether you're splashing down a river or caught in an afternoon shower while hiking, expect to get wet. Bag, then double-bag, all your equipment in plastic. Camera, food, clothing, and especially your sleeping bag need protection.

In years of soaking rainstorms and intimate encounters with rivers, I've never gotten my down-filled sleeping bag wet. Here's how to keep your bag dry. First, stuff the sleeping bag into a nylon stuff sack. The stuff sack doesn't need to be waterproof. Next, put the stuff sack inside a heavy three-mil plastic bag. Secure the plastic bag's opening by twisting it tightly, folding it over, then wrapping it with a heavy rubber band. If you will be taking a paddling trip, repeat this process with a second plastic bag. Finally, place the whole thing inside a second, slightly larger, nylon stuff sack. Even if your down bag is carried on the outside of your pack, it will be protected from both water and abrasion.

Home-Dried One-Pot Meals

". . . in the woods, eating is what counts most in life."

—Norman Maclean, *USFS 1919: The Ranger, the Cook, and a Hole in the Sky*, 1976

When your appetite has been sharpened by fresh air and exercise, good food is the highlight of your day. At the end of the day, you're hungry for a delicious, filling, hot meal, but you don't want to cook. Cooking is fun when you're at home with all the conveniences of a modern kitchen, but elaborate meal preparations in camp are tedious.

Here's how you can enjoy tasty, memorable meals while camping, without cooking in camp. Dehydrate your own complete portable meals at home before you go camping. Keep a supply of ready-to-pack meals on hand for last-minute trips. Home-dried gourmet meals are economical, tasty, and lightweight, and they require no cooking, just heating, in the field. Best of all, you can choose the foods you enjoy most and the portions are generous.

> **Enjoy tasty and memorable meals while camping without cooking in camp by dehydrating complete portable meals at home before you go camping.**

If you don't own an electric dehydrator with a heat source and a fan, borrow one from a friend or relative. Many people who own dehydrators don't realize that they can do much more with them than simply dry sliced fruit and vegetables. Use the recipes and instructions in this book to create your own one-pot meals. Since the dehydrator does the work, you'll find it easy to dry complete meals at home for later enjoyment while on vacation.

Drying is an ancient method of food preservation requiring no preservatives. It's a simple concept: heat and air circulation remove most of the moisture from the food. The lack of moisture keeps microorganisms from growing and spoiling the food.

Soups, stews, and casseroles are the best choices for dehydrated meals because the ingredients can be chopped or sliced into small pieces for quick drying. Dry soups, stews, and casseroles quickly and easily in a dehydrator for safe, high-quality meals.

Completely cook your meal at home. For example, you can easily prepare a dehydrated spaghetti dinner. First, make your favorite meat, seafood, or vegetable sauce, or heat some commer-

cial sauce. Then cook and drain your choice of fresh or dried pasta. Finally, mix together the warm sauce and the warm, drained pasta. Place sheets of plastic wrap over the middle of the dehydrator trays, leaving an inch or two of space between the edge of the plastic wrap and the edge of the dehydrator tray, for better air circulation. Spread the spaghetti dinner on the plastic-covered trays. Turn your dehydrator to its highest temperature setting, 145° F on most dehydrators. Dry the spaghetti for about 4 to 6

Spread the food on plastic-covered dehydrator trays.

hours. While the food is drying, check it once every hour or so if possible. To check the food, first scrub and dry your hands. Using your fingers, turn and break up the food. If you see any large, moist pieces of food, crumble them to help the food dry more evenly. The food is dry when it looks and feels dry, crunchy, and crumbly. If it feels moist, dry it a little longer.

High-quality commercial dehydrators, such as Excalibur Products (6083 Power Inn Road, Sacramento, CA 95824, (800) 875-4254) or Nesco American Harvest (4064 Peavey Road, Chaska, MN 55318, (800) 288-4545) are very foolproof. They make home-drying of complete meals easy. If you are unable to check and turn the food a few times while

Soups, stews, and casseroles are the best choices for dehydrated meals because the ingredients can be chopped or sliced into small pieces for quick drying.

> If you store your dehydrated one-pot meals in heavy, black plastic bags in the refrigerator, they will keep for up to 2 years or, if stored in the freezer, they will keep for 3 or more years.

it is drying, these dehydrators are forgiving. It is almost impossible to overdry or otherwise ruin your home-dried meals.

Turn off the dehydrator. Let the food stand for several hours or overnight to cool completely. The next morning, your dried meals will be ready to package. Place the dried, cooled meals in small, sturdy plastic bags. Seal the bags well, squeezing out as much air as possible, then double-bag them in a second plastic bag, inserting a label between the two bags. Write on the label the name of the recipe, how many people it will serve, today's date, and instructions for rehydrating the meal. All of your home-dried meals will have the same rehydrating instructions: cover with water, boil, stir, and serve.

Dried meals store well for a long time if you keep them cool, dark, and dry. For the best quality,

You can dry complete meals in a dehydrator.

keep your meals in heavy, black plastic bags in the refrigerator for up to 2 years or in the freezer for 3 or more years. The meals can be stored at room temperature in a cool, dark, dry location in your house or in your vehicle, boat, or backpack, but they will retain their highest quality if refrigerated or frozen. When it's time to take a camping trip, store the meals in your vehicle, boat, or backpack. Bagged in their black plastic bag in a cool, dark, dry place, they will keep for months.

In the field, your one-pot meals are quickly rehydrated. Cover the food with water, bring it to a boil, stir, serve, and enjoy. The only field equipment you will need is a lightweight aluminum pot with a lid, a stove, fuel, and one Sierra cup and aluminum spoon per person.

> **In camp, cover the food with water, bring it to a boil, stir, serve, and enjoy.**

When it's time to serve dinner, fill your Sierra cup with hot food. You do not need to carry a cup and a bowl and a plate. One Sierra cup does the job of all three. Since it is made of stainless steel, it can be placed on or near your stove or campfire to keep food warm while the cup handle remains cool enough to touch. It is indestructible. One cup will last you a lifetime. Other metal dishware can be too hot to touch, even when you simply serve hot soup or coffee in it.

A thermal cup made of Lexan plastic is another good choice for an all-purpose camping cup/bowl/plate. These cups keep food warm, even in very cold temperatures, but of course they cannot be heated like metal, nor do they last as long. Lexan thermal cups are a superb choice for tea or coffee on frosty winter mornings in camp, and they will keep your dinner hot when you are snow camping.

Place a label between the plastic bags that identifies the food.

Campfires

Learn how to build a safe, efficient campfire, then build one only when the situation is appropriate. Campfires are time-consuming, and they pollute the air as well as campers. Portable stoves are easier to control than campfires. Stoves are more efficient for cooking because they heat evenly and quickly. Campfires disperse heat unevenly. Fires can give off sparks, particularly dangerous near clothing or other equipment made of nylon or other synthetics. Campfires also attract unwelcome creatures such as bears intent on raiding your food supply.

Sometimes campfires are appropriate, necessary, or simply extremely desirable. They can even be lifesaving. Be prepared. Practice your fire-building proficiency, but always use caution and good judgment before you light up.

Request a free campfire permit from any forestry office, in person or by mail, before your camping trip. You will need a permit to use either an outdoor stove or a wood or charcoal campfire. Permits are good for one calendar year. You are responsible for learning and following the general fire regulations for the area as well as the special limitations that are in force at the time you'll be visiting. Regulations are more stringent during times of high fire danger, and these restrictions are strictly enforced. A folding shovel and a bucket may be required equipment when using a campfire.

Burn only dead, downed wood. Gather downed wood some distance from your campsite to avoid stripping the landscape in popular areas. Use only existing fire rings sited on nonburnable mineral soil. Clear the area of leaves and needles. Very wet or

Sierra cup and aluminum spoon

porous rocks can explode when they are heated to a high temperature, so keep them away from your fire. Before you light your campfire, assemble everything you need: food, cooking gear, and burnables such as paper, kindling, and the fuel you will need to sustain the fire. Keep your campfire neat and small. Don't walk away from it, even for a few minutes.

After you have used your campfire, drown it with plenty of water. Stir the drowned fire, then drown it and stir it again. The

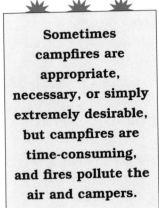

Sometimes campfires are appropriate, necessary, or simply extremely desirable, but campfires are time-consuming, and fires pollute the air and campers.

If you must make a campfire, use only dead, downed wood from a wide area around your campsite.

remains of your fire must be cold to the touch before you leave it.

Clean up after your fire. Naturalize the area. Pack out every bit of your own and anyone else's garbage you come across.

Storing Food

Protect all foods, fresh or dried, from heat and moisture. Bag, then double-bag everything in black plastic bags. Keep all your food cool, dark, and dry.

In your vehicle, protect your food from tiny rodents that can even squeeze into your car through the hole under the brake pedal. Food tins are mouseproof, as are heavy, tightly sealed plastic containers. Ask restaurants for their reusable discards.

Keep fragile foods such as crackers, cookies, bread, or cake slices from breaking while you're on the trail. Scrub some used waxed milk or juice cartons, then dry them thoroughly. Fill the cartons with individually bagged servings of fragile foods. Place the cartons in large plastic bags. Flatten and pack out the cartons when they're empty.

Hard cheese keeps well without refrigeration if you protect it from heat,

Pack fragile food in waxed milk cartons.

mold, and dryness. Most soft cheese must be refrigerated. Read the
label before you buy. For long camping trips, select dense, hard,
natural cheese such as Cheddar, Parmesan, Romano, or dry Monterey Jack. If your cheese is not wax-covered, protect it from mold
during long or warm-weather trips. Dip a piece of cheesecloth in a
mixture of five parts water to one part distilled white vinegar (or
another variety). Wring the cloth thoroughly. Wrap the cheese in
plastic wrap, then wrap the plastic-covered cheese with the vinegar-
dampened cheesecloth. Double-bag the whole thing in heavy plastic bags. Store cheese in a cool, dark location while camping.

Counterbalance Food

*He was the biggest bear we had ever seen, yet he moved as
quickly as a cat. He snatched our neighboring campers' bag
of sugar treats. We watched in awe as the bear swallowed the
whole five-pound bag, including many layers of plastic, in
one tremendous gulp.*

✳   ✳   ✳

Don't let your trip be marred by an unwelcome bear encounter.
Bears do not want to tangle with you. They just want to eat the
food you are carrying. Here are some suggestions for protecting
your precious camping food supply.

- Ask rangers about local bear conditions. Follow their advice.
  Be conservative.
- This is the most secure way to store food in bear country: buy
  or rent bearproof aluminum containers from camping stores
  or national parks. These containers are just large enough to
  carry dehydrated meals for a backpack trip. Use the larger, sta-

tionary bearproof lockers found at some campgrounds and at popular backcountry tent camp sites.

- If you must store food in your vehicle, put it in the trunk of your car. Bears can pop out your vehicle's windows, or pry off your camper shell if they are able to hook their claws into even a tiny crack.

- Don't cook in or near your tent. Use the one-pot home-dried meal recipes included in this book to cook and dehydrate your meals ahead of time. Then, when you're in camp, your food will heat quickly and create little odor. Avoid campfires. Bacon cooking on a campfire will attract every bear in the region.

- Always store food well away from your tent and cook a good distance away, in another direction, from both your sleeping and eating areas.

- At popular people-wise bear sites such as national parks that do not have bearproof lockers, don't bring odoriferous foods. Seal your food well in plastic bags to keep the odors contained. Store the plastic bags several feet up off the ground, on boulders, well away from your tent. Weight the bags with rocks. This method may keep bears from seeing or smelling the food.

- In the remote backcountry, counterbalance your food from a high tree limb. Take time to

Black Bear

find the right tree. If you are in bear territory, you will find an appropriate tree. (Bears do not live in treeless settings, such as high alpine zones or open desert.) Select a lone, healthy tree limb. It must be 17 to 20 feet off the ground and strong enough to hold your food bags, but too weak to support a curious bear cub.

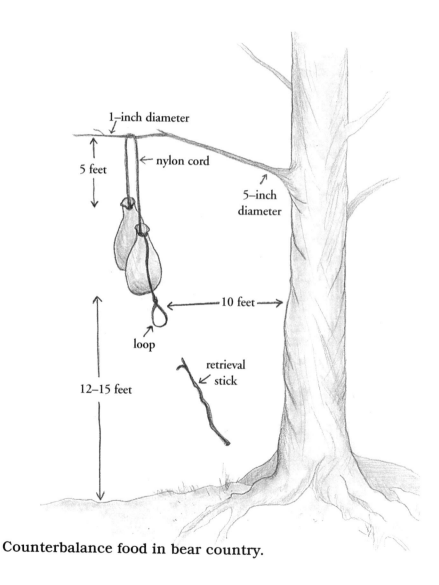

Counterbalance food in bear country.

- Divide food into two bags of equal weight. Besides all of your food, place your garbage bag, toothpaste, soap, lotions, and anything else that is odoriferous in these two bags. Tie a rock to the end of a 50-foot length

> **Bacon cooking on a campfire will attract every bear in the region.**

of nylon cord and throw the rock over the limb. Remove the rock. Tie the first bag to the cord in place of the rock.

Pull the first bag all the way up to the branch. Tie the second bag as high on the cord as you can reach. Tie a loop of cord hanging from the top of the second bag; this loop will help you retrieve the bags later. Using a forked stick, push the second bag up, next to the first bag.

To retrieve the bags, use the forked stick to hook the loop of cord. Carefully pull the bags down.

Take care to cook and store your food responsibly. If you leave food or trash strewn around your camp, you may cause a bear to be destroyed. Wild creatures that taste human food can become aggressive hunted animals. Don't be responsible for a bear's death.

Safe, Plentiful Drinking Water

When you're living outdoors, keep water, extra water containers, and water treatment handy. Since you need to drink often, before you are thirsty, make it easy to keep yourself hydrated. Bring treated water from home. Store at least 5 to 10 gallons of treated water in your vehicle when you camp. At every opportunity, replenish your supply with water that has been properly treated.

Never drink untreated water. Contaminated water may look clean and taste good because Giardia lamblia and other microscopic bacteria are invisible and tasteless. *Giardia lamblia* is a tiny one-celled parasite that can cause long-lasting illness. The unpleasant symptoms of illness caused by Giardia include diarrhea, cramps, gas, fatigue, and weight loss. Giardia is prevalent worldwide. In recent years, Giardia has become common in streams, rivers, and lakes throughout North America. Giardia is spread by drinking water that has been contaminated by the feces of animals or careless outdoorspeople.

To protect yourself from waterborne illness, choose one or a combination of the following water treatment options:

- *Boil* untreated water for 3 minutes before using it for drinking, cooking, or brushing your teeth. Next to bringing treated water from home, boiling is the safest method of water treatment. If the water contains bits of dirt and bark, filter it through a cloth before boiling it. The boiling method of water treatment is time-consuming. When you are thirsty, the hot water seems to take forever to cool down, and boiled water tastes flat. When you are staying in a base camp, take time to boil extra water during the evening for use the next day. When you are backpacking, paddling, or otherwise on the move, you won't want to stop several times during the day to boil your drinking water. If you are using a portable stove, you will need to carry extra fuel. Boiling is a lightweight method of water treatment if you are using a wood campfire since no extra equipment is required. Boiling is a very safe method of water treatment.

- *Filter* water through a portable microporous (microstrainer) filter, which quickly turns even murky, questionable water into good-tasting drinking water. When shopping for a portable water filter, check with the Centers for Disease Control and Prevention for information on current brands. Look for a filter with pore sizes of less than 1 micrometer, to filter out Giardia cysts. Buy a filter that can be effectively cleaned and replaced when needed. Select a filter with a pumping capacity that is appropriate for most of your needs. A very small filter is lightweight. It is perfect for one or two people who enjoy backpacking. Larger camping parties will want a bigger, heavier filter that can produce greater quantities of water per minute of pumping. If you are traveling to parts of the world where water-borne viruses may be a problem, use iodine tablets in addition to your microporous filter. First filter the raw water, then add water treatment tablets and let

portable water filter

stand for 30 to 60 minutes, or overnight. A filter slightly increases the weight of your pack, but weighs much less than a quart-sized canteen full of water.

- *Iodine* or *chlorine* added to untreated water are less reliable than boiling or filtering, but they do give you some protection against Giardia, and they will destroy most bacteria and viruses that cause illness. Consider iodine or chlorine as substitutes when you cannot boil or filter your water, and as a supplement in addition to filtering your water in parts of the world where waterborne viruses are a threat. Add to 1 quart of untreated water: 5 to 10 drops of 2-percent tincture of iodine, or 2 to 4 drops of 4- to 6-percent liquid chlorine bleach, or use tiny, lightweight commercial tablets. Shake to mix thoroughly, then let stand for 30 to 60 minutes, or overnight. Cold water requires longer contact time than warm water. Be patient and let the water stand. Longer contact time will give the iodine time to work, and the longer the water stands, the better it will taste. Improve the flavor of chemically treated water by adding lightweight tablets that eliminate the taste of iodine. Potable Aqua treatment tablets, used with P.A. Plus added 20 minutes after the first tablets, effectively erase the unpleasant flavor. Alternatively, disguise the taste with powdered drink mix.

Protect Water Sources

Keep streams pristine and protect yourself and others from disease. Don't wash yourself, your clothes, or your dishes in any open water source. Using a clean jug or bucket, dip water from a creek, lake, or river. Carry the water at least 200 feet away from the water source to your washing-up spot. Use little or no soap. If you cook with home-dried one-pot meals, cooking pots will hold almost no food residue; they can be cleaned with a quick wipe using a piece of nylon net material. Clothing, too, can be cleaned with little or no soap. Agitating clothes in water, then drying them in the sun and wind, is quite effective. Dispose of your wash water properly. Distribute it over an area located at least 200 feet away from any water source, seasonal watercourse, trail, or campsite.

Human Waste Disposal

To prevent the spread of diseases such as Giardia lamblia, E. coli, and hepatitis A and B, dispose of your waste responsibly. In wooded areas with diggable topsoil, practice cat sanitation. Find a secluded spot 200 feet or more from any water source, seasonal watercourse, campsite, or trail. Dig a hole in the topsoil 6 to 8 inches deep. Wipe yourself with a smooth leaf or as little toilet paper as possible. If you use toilet paper, burn it when you're done, and make sure the fire is extinguished. Stir the waste with a stick to aid decomposition, then fill in the hole with soil and naturalize the site with leaves and twigs.

> **Find a new site for your personal toilet place each time and place a twig X or other agreed-upon symbol to mark your spot.**

If you're camping with a group, mark each personal toilet place with a twig X or other agreed-upon sign. All members of the party need to find a new site each time.

In steep river canyons, boat campers need to bring a portable group latrine or use individual poop tubes for ultralight trips, if they can't get away from the river-banks.

Always clean your hands after defecating. Keep a supply of premoistened wipes handy in an outside pocket of your pack. Premoistened wipes must be packed out, but they are convenient, compact, and very lightweight. Wash with soap and water in camp during the mornings and evenings, when you have a washing area set up, then use premoistened wipes during the day.

Sleep Comfortably

Choose a nearly level tent site, away from all potential water drainage courses and possible falling objects such as boulders, dead trees or tree limbs, or large pine cones. If the site is not quite level, place your tent so you will sleep with your head uphill. Carefully clear the area of sharp rocks and twigs. Replace the rocks and twigs when you break camp, so the site remains natural-looking.

> **When you camp on sand, gravel, or snow, carefully scoop out slight depressions for your hips and shoulders before setting up your ground cloth and tent.**

When you camp on sand, gravel, or snow, carefully scoop out slight depressions for your hips and shoulders before setting up your ground cloth and tent. You will sleep more comfortably and feel less stiff in the morning when you rest on a surface whose contours mimic the shape of your body. Do not disturb the soil. Replace the sand or gravel after you break camp.

A ground cloth pro-
tects the bottom of your tent from water, dirt, and punctures. However, during a heavy rainstorm, a ground cloth that is larger than

ground cloth

your tent floor can turn the inside of the tent into a pond. Rain will accumulate under the tent and pool in the ground cloth. The water will then soak through your tent floor, no matter how waterproof the fabric.

To prevent pooling of water under your tent, fold the edges of the ground cloth under the tent. The ground cloth must be well under the tent, out of sight, so rain can't reach it and collect in it. If you are expecting a lot of rain or will be camping on snow, pack a second, larger ground cloth. Use it inside the tent. This ground cloth should be large enough to run up the tent walls a few inches. Even when you're camping on snow, or sleeping through an all-night rainstorm, this interior ground cloth will ensure a warm, dry night.

> **Replace the sand or gravel after you break camp.**

Prevent Hypothermia

Every year unprepared people die from exposure to cold. Often they are on a simple day hike in air temperatures of only 40° to 50° F. Hypothermia strikes when your body temperature drops below about 95° F. Wind, rain, or submersion in water can lower your body's core temperature very quickly.

Constantly adjust your layers of clothing. Don't let yourself become either chilled or soaked with perspiration. Drink water and eat frequent snacks. Monitor yourself and your companions for these signs: chills, shivering, lethargy, poor coordination, or irrationality. Take immediate action. Stop and seek whatever shelter is available to you. If you do not have a tent, seek the most protected area you can find. Remove wet clothing. Put on all available dry clothing. Cover your head and neck, since more than half of the body's heat can be lost through the head. Warm your companions with blankets or a sleeping bag. If you have no bedding, get them inside a large plastic bag or under piles of branches and leaves. Warm your companions with skin-to-skin body heat, then give them hot water or soup.

> A hat with a wide brim of 3 or more inches and a high crown will keep you cooler or warmer.

Protect Your Skin and Eyes

Prevent sunburn and conserve your body's water supply. Cover all exposed skin with cool, light-colored clothing. Water-repellent sunscreen of at least 15 SPF needs to be applied, and reapplied, liberally. Apply sunscreen to all exposed areas, preferably an hour before you go outdoors. Use lip balm containing sunscreen. Zinc ointment, an opaque cream, very effectively protects the nose and lips.

When you're on the water, on sand, or on snow, glaring sunlight is assaulting you from all directions. In these situations, glacier glasses with dark, ultraviolet-ray-blocking lenses and side shields are your best protection. Wear your regular sunglasses while driving to and from the trailhead because glacier glasses do restrict a driver's peripheral vision. Look for a high UV (ultraviolet) rating when buying regular sunglasses or glacier glasses.

A hat with a wide brim of 3 or more inches and a high crown will keep you cooler or warmer. It will protect your face, neck, and that delicate area on top of your head where the sun beats down hardest and where everyone's hair is thinner. Don't go outdoors without a hat.

Wide-brimmed hat with a chin strap

Select a hat made of tough packable cotton or synthetic. It must have a chin strap or you'll lose it in the river while running white water or on a windy mountaintop. You can add a chin strap to your hat by sewing a length of loose, comfortable ¼-inch-wide flat or round cord elastic to the inside of the hat band, just in front of your ears.

Glacier glasses are not just for hiking on glaciers.

Avoid Dehydration and Heatstroke

When you are living outdoors, drink much more water than you think you need. Three to six quarts of water per day are required by the average adult. In extreme conditions—such as hiking in hot, open desert—up to 3 gallons of water per person per day are needed. This is a tremendous amount of water and a tremendous amount of weight if you must carry it. One gallon of water weighs 8½ pounds.

If you need to carry all your water while camping in waterless country, your need for liquid will obviously restrict your camping options. Plan your water stops beforehand. Cache water in advance if necessary. Look for watercourses on your topographic (commonly referred to as topo) maps, and be sure the watercourses you see on the maps contain water year-round if you are camping during a dry season. A topo map will also indicate the shape of the land showing altitude changes, the ruggedness of the terrain, and vegetation. (See Maps in Chapter 2 for a more detailed description of topo maps.)

Sometimes you may not even notice that you are becoming dehydrated. Take care to drink enough water when the temperatures are cool, when you are in or on the water, or are exercising vigorously in the snow.

Drink water before you feel thirsty. Water carried in your canteen doesn't help you; a container of drinking water is "better in you than on you." Once you have become dehydrated it takes much more water to become adequately rehydrated than it would if you had kept drinking steadily all along. Monitor yourself and your companions for these warning signs: no need to urinate, lack of perspiration, hot dry skin, labored breathing, dizziness, nausea, stomach or muscle cramps. Get into the shade, rest, drink water, and bathe skin with cool water, but don't immerse the person in cold water because this can cause shock. Below is a concoction that can help replenish your bodily fluids.

Rehydration Drink

1 cup serving

7½ ounces cool water

1 tablespoon sugar

1 tablespoon fruit juice or 1 teaspoon powdered fruit
   juice mix

⅛ teaspoon salt

Lightning

*The sky blackened. Our hair literally stood on end. We were
on the shoulder of a mountain and watched as the 12,000-*

foot peak was lit repeatedly by lightning. We stayed in light-ning position as the storm swept past. Wearing our rubber-soled boots, we crouched on our foam sleeping pads, touch-ing nothing. Only the soles of our boots were in contact with the foam pads and the ground beneath them.

✳   ✳   ✳

Keep an eye out for approaching storms. Take cover. Get off peaks and ridges. Land your boat and stay well away from any water.

The storm swept past.

Maintain a low profile. Minimize your height. Keep away from all tall trees or land masses, and away from anything metallic. Minimize your contact with the ground, so ground currents have less chance to run through your body.

Ticks

Ticks love humans. They lie in wait in the grass, in shrubs, and in trees. Ticks hitchhike onto humans from the undergrowth, then seek a choice feeding place: your groin, behind your knees, or in your armpits. They are especially prevalent during the months of May and June, when new vegetation flourishes. While hiking in dense growth, take special care to protect your arms and legs. Wear long-sleeved shirts and trousers, and use gaiters or elastic bands to protect your ankles. Apply insect repellent to your clothing. While living outdoors, make it a habit to inspect yourself and your companions for ticks at least once a day.

If a tick becomes imbedded in your skin, don't touch it. First, loosen it by covering it with petroleum jelly, or use a tissue or piece of cotton soaked in rubbing alcohol. Wait several minutes. The tick will either pull out of your skin because it is smothering, or it will die and become limp. Then use fine-pointed tweezers to carefully pull off the entire tick. Wash the area with soap and water. If the tick's head remains imbedded in your skin, seek medical attention. Ticks can carry serious diseases such as Rocky Mountain Spotted Fever and Lyme disease. Some signs of Lyme disease include flulike symptoms and muscle and head pain. Seek medical attention if you have been bitten by a tick, or if any of these symptoms appear after you have been in tick country.

> **While living outdoors, make it a habit to inspect yourself and your companions for ticks at least once a day.**

Instant Gaiters

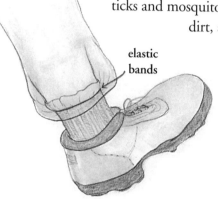

elastic
bands

Use elastic bands to create "gaiters." These bands will keep ticks and mosquitoes off your legs and help keep brush, dirt, and water out of your socks.

Put comfortable rubber bands, or lengths of elastic, around your ankles, over your socks. Pull your trouser legs down over the bands, then fold them up, tucking the ends of the trousers underneath the elastic bands.

Elastic-band gaiters will help keep ticks off your skin.

Mosquitoes

Cover up. Wear a hat. Wear a fine-mesh nylon head net over the hat when bugs are unbearable. A head net cuts down a bit on visibility, but it's worth it when the mosquitoes are really biting. You can easily hike, even off-trail, while wearing a head net.

Loose-fitting clothing protects you best. The insects can bite your skin through tight-fitting clothes. Wear two layers of clothing, with light-colored clothing on the outside. Dark colors, such as navy blue and black, attract mosquitoes. Instead of dark colors, choose white, beige, or other pale colors.

Avoid scented soaps, perfumes, deodorants, or body lotions; floral scents can attract a variety of flying insects. Camp in open, breezy areas, well away from water. Apply insect repellent to your hat, scarf, and shirt cuffs rather than directly to your skin. Camp in potentially buggy areas only during the driest months of the year. Remember that mosquitoes mean wilderness; they do help keep wild areas uncrowded and let you enjoy the solitude.

Snakes

In our area, the western foothills of the Sierra Nevada, prime Western Rattlesnake country, we rarely spot these handsome creatures. During the balmy month of May, they may be seen sunning themselves. When the weather is very cold or very hot, the rattlesnakes remain under cover and out of sight. Bites from poisonous snakes in North America rarely cause death. Prevent surprise snake encounters by never putting your hand somewhere you can't see it or stepping somewhere you can't see where your foot will land. While camping in snake country, keep your tent zipped up and don't walk around at night. Wear proper boots. Sweep the trail in front of you with your eyes, back and forth. If bitten, keep quiet and comfortable and get medical attention as soon as possible.

Poison Oak, Poison Ivy, and Sumac

Learn to recognize and avoid poisonous plants. Be alert, especially while practicing cat sanitation. Look for the leaflets in groups of three that are found on both poison oak and poison ivy plants. "Leaves of three, let it be." Don't touch any parts of these plants, and don't burn any part of them in a campfire. The smoke can not only cause skin rash and swelling, but it can also damage your lungs.

If you think you have touched these plants, wash the affected parts of your body with water—no soap—as soon as possible. Try to wash within 10 minutes of your exposure to the plants. This would be a good time for a quick swim in a creek, letting the water rush over your skin. Most

> **If you think you have touched poison ivy, poison oak, or sumac, wash the affected parts of your body with water—no soap—as soon as possible.**

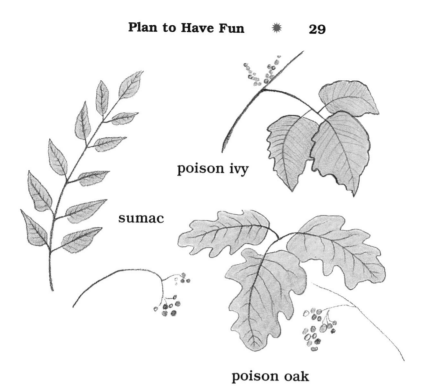

poison ivy

sumac

poison oak

important, remove any clothing that might have brushed against the poisonous plants. Try not to touch the clothing. Use a stick to push the clothing into a plastic bag. Seal the bag and wash the clothing thoroughly when you get home.

Calamine lotion will reduce the itching caused by skin rashes. Carry a small plastic bottle of calamine lotion if you'll be camping for any length of time in areas where these poisonous plants are prevalent. Antihistamine tablets may provide some relief. Seek medical attention for serious cases.

Safety Preparedness

A certified first aid training course, including cardiopulmonary resuscitation, should be taken, and retaken annually, by all campers. For training courses, contact the American Red Cross, the Sierra Club, the American Heart Association, or other local

> **Antihistamine tablets may provide some relief from poison ivy, poison oak, or sumac.**

groups. First aid training and a concise portable reference guide will help you decide what to do—and not do—in an emergency.

Most minor wilderness medical problems do not require elaborate first aid. Prompt washing with soap and flushing with plenty of water is the best way to clean most cuts. Immediate immersion in cold water, then application of some 2nd Skin from your foot kit, will soothe minor first-degree burns (see foot kit in Backpack List, Chapter 2). When faced with major medical problems, basic knowledge of first aid will help you to assess the victim's condition. If the injured person is not breathing or is bleeding severely, you must use your knowledge to give him or her immediate treatment, then treat the person for shock and provide comfort—without moving him or her. Your training will help you make the next important decision: evacuate the ill or injured person yourself, or go seek professional help. First aid courses will help you remain calm, make a good decision, and not make things worse.

Prevention of accidents is your best defense. Remain alert. Observe your companions closely. Do they appear chilled or overtired? Stop moving and take care of any members of your party who need attention. Move cautiously. Don't rush or make hasty decisions. Play "what if" games with your companions and while you are alone. Discuss emergency exit routes from the wilderness, and know where staffed backcountry ranger stations are located. Visualize your reaction in emergency situations. Read accounts of survival in the wilderness to sharpen your awareness. We humans are physically fragile and susceptible to heat and cold, but we have the ability to collect our thoughts and analyze. We're survivors.

> **Design your adventure to best take advantage of each person's knowledge and strengths, and cater to everyone's interests.**

Party size is an important safety consideration. Take solo trips only with great caution. Three people is the minimum party size for a safe adventure in the wilderness. If one person is injured while far from a vehicle or trailhead, the second person can stay with the victim while the third goes for help. A party of four, with two people traveling together to seek help, is even safer. Always consider the strengths and weaknesses of all of your party's members. Don't attempt a camping trip that is beyond the ability of your weakest member. Design your adventure to best take advantage of each person's knowledge and strengths, and cater to everyone's interests.

Check Vehicle, Share Trip Plan

**"Make sure you got extries,"
warned the old desert rat. "Extry food,
extry water, an' a' extry tire."**

A few basics may save your life in an emergency, and will enable you to camp almost anywhere, because you are self-contained.

Before your wilderness trip, make sure your vehicle is tuned and in good repair. Carry at least a tool kit, extra drinking water, motor oil, jumper cables, and a properly inflated spare tire. A folding shovel and a couple of strips of carpet will help you extricate your vehicle from snow, mud, or sand.

Before you head out on a remote trip, give a trusted friend or relative your trip plan. Copy your map for them and highlight the route. Indicate on the map where you might camp each night. Tell your friend that if she hasn't seen or heard from you by a certain date and time, you are in trouble. Then, if everything goes as planned and you return home safely, make sure you contact your friend before this date and time.

> **Before you head out on a remote trip, give a trusted friend or relative at home your trip plan.**

Extra Change of Warm Clothes

Here in California, tourists wearing their warm-climate clothes routinely drive from mild-climate regions of the state to the much colder mountain elevations. When their car breaks down during cold or wet weather, they are unprepared. Wherever you live, and in whatever season you travel, always carry in your vehicle emergency clothes, protected in a plastic bag, and footwear you can walk in.

If you return to your vehicle soaking wet and cold after a day of hiking, you'll be glad to slip into dry, warm clothes. Don't forget to pack long underwear, even in summer. We've been caught in snow, during July and August, at higher mountain elevations and in far northern latitudes. Long underwear makes wonderful pajamas or emergency garb if your clothes get wet. Medium-weight synthetic long underwear is fast-drying, comfortable in most temperatures, and rolls up compactly in your backpack, boat, or vehicle. Protect long underwear from dampness by storing it in a plastic bag.

Trousers

Heavy cotton denim jeans protect your skin when you are walking through brushy country or sliding on rocks. They are, however, hot in hot weather and cold in cold weather. On a frosty morning, denim jeans may be so stiff they are hard to put on. If you get them wet, they can remain so for days, and they can chafe your skin. For more comfortable outdoor adventures, try the following substitutes for your favorite blue jeans.

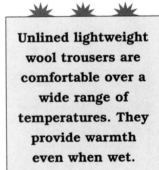

Unlined lightweight wool trousers are comfortable over a wide range of temperatures. They provide warmth even when wet.

- *Unlined lightweight wool trousers* are comfortable over a wide range of temperatures. They provide warmth even when wet, although they do not dry as quickly as trousers made of synthetic fabrics. They are softer and more comfortable to climb into on a cold morning than jeans. Wool trousers are a good all-around camping choice during fairly dry weather in open terrain when temperatures are mild to cold.

- *Well-broken-in cotton duck or twill trousers* are more comfortable than jeans. In a medium-weight fabric, they give you much of the same protection against sharp brush and rocks, but they feel softer and cooler. They are a good choice for backpacking. If medium-weight cotton trousers get wet during a stream-crossing, they dry more quickly than jeans do.

For paddling trips, hiking trips with many river crossings, and hot weather trips, try *lightweight nylon trousers*. They are cool, comfortable, and almost weightless. They dry very quickly. Lightweight nylon fabric is not as warm as cotton or wool. When the evening turns cold, wear your long underwear underneath the trousers. Lightweight nylon is the perfect fabric choice for desert hiking or warm-weather paddling trips.

> **Try lightweight nylon trousers for paddling trips, hiking trips with many river crossings, and hot-weather trips.**

- *Heavier weight nylon or other synthetic fabric trousers* are designed for climbing, hiking, and paddling. They offer excellent resistance to brush and rocks. Nylon trousers dry quickly and are comfortable over a wide range of temperatures. They are a good choice for any outdoor adventure.

- Always carry a pair of *lightweight nylon shorts*. When the weather turns hot, when you need to wade across a stream, or when your trousers get wet, change into your shorts. When you're camping light, leave your extra pair of trousers at home and pack a pair of running shorts instead.

Be Good to Your Feet

Just before you leave on your camping trip, protect any known trouble spots on your feet with moleskin, New-Skin liquid bandages, or adhesive foam pads. A blister can disable you and spoil your camping adventure. Prevent blisters by treating your feet year-round. While you're on the trail, don't be a martyr. Pay attention to trouble signals, and take care of foot problems immediately. Your blister could ruin the whole camping party's trip.

Here are some year-round foot-care tips.

- Keep a bottle of rubbing alcohol next to your home shower or bathtub. Year-round, rub your feet with alcohol after each shower, paying special attention to your toes and heels. The regular use of rubbing alcohol toughens skin, making it more resistant to blisters.

> **Treat your feet to cooling alcohol rubs while hiking.**

- Go barefoot at home.
- Walk regularly.
- Treat your feet to cooling alcohol rubs while hiking, and don't go on any outing without your foot kit (see Backpack List, Chapter 2).

Wrap some micropore tape around the moleskin or pads, if needed, to hold them in place. This protection will last for days, and you may avert trouble while camping.

At the first sign of foot discomfort while hiking, stop and assess the problem. Don't continue hiking if you feel the slightest twinge of a potential blister. Reach for your foot kit. Treat and protect the tender area of skin before it becomes a blister. Take off your boots and socks and locate the sore spot. Clean it with water, a premoistened wipe, or rubbing alcohol, then apply a piece of moleskin or liquid bandage. Cover the moleskin with micropore tape, if necessary, to keep it in place.

If a small, flat blister forms, simply clean it with water and rubbing alcohol and protect it by applying a piece of 2nd Skin. Do not apply moleskin to a blister. To prevent infection, it's best to leave the blister intact. If a large blister has formed, you may need to drain it. To drain the blister, sterilize a needle by holding it in a match's flame, then letting it cool. Gently puncture the blister near its lower edge and let it drain. Clean the area with water and rubbing alcohol and cover it with a piece of 2nd Skin. Watch the blister carefully over the next few days. If needed, clean it, redrain it, and change the dressing.

rubbing alcohol

Take only your best-fitting socks on your adventures. Socks that are too large will ruck and cause blisters. Those that are too small will constrict toes. Since sock sizes vary, test the size before you buy. In the store, make a fist of one hand. With your other hand, wrap the foot of the sock around the widest part of your fist. The sock's toe and heel should just meet. Check your socks carefully for worn spots before you pack them. Hiking is hard on socks, so you'll want to begin your trip with socks that are in excellent condition.

Wear two layers of socks, one pair of thin liner socks made of synthetic or silk

> ✴ ✴ ✴
> **Test the size of a sock by making a fist with one hand. With the other, wrap the foot of the sock around the widest part of your fist. If the toe and heel meet, the socks should fit.**

material plus a pair of heavy outer socks. The liner socks wick away moisture and help prevent blisters. The outer socks provide padding, protection, and insulation. For your outer layer, choose socks designed specifically for hiking. Thick wool or synthetic socks, or those made of a blend of wool and synthetic, wick away perspiration and provide warmth even when they are wet. Cotton socks do not meet these requirements.

Keep adjusting your boots and socks. Socks tend to sag and ruck. On the trail, bits of dirt work their way inside of boots and socks. Solve these problems by frequently taking off your boots and socks and shaking them out. Smooth the socks carefully over your feet when you replace them. Rough trails loosen bootlaces. Keep adjusting your laces for the most comfortable, suppportive fit possible.

hiking socks

Be an Expert with Your Equipment

As we rounded the shoulder of Mt. Linn, the snowstorm bore down on us unexpectedly. The winds reached gale force in a matter of minutes. Without a word, we dropped our backpacks and quickly wrestled the tent into place, throwing the packs inside before we tumbled in ourselves, panting with exertion.

✳   ✳   ✳

Know how to set up your tent quickly. Don't be caught perusing the tent's instruction manual when the storm hits, or try to light your stove for the very first time while on a wilderness camping trip. Let each adult member of your party practice using your equipment at home. Everyone should know where all the equipment is stored in camp and how to use it properly.

Keep all of your equipment as clean and dry as possible, and protect it from strains, tears, and breakage. Shake, then sponge off or air dry your tent and fly before packing them from one campsite to another. When you reach your new camp, set up your tent and fly. They will finish drying quickly. Take advantage of good weather. Use the sun and wind to dry out wet clothing and equipment whenever you can.

Most modern tents are quick to assemble and stake, but they must be handled with common sense. If you do not weight down your freestanding tent while you are assembling it, the tent can turn into a big kite, sailing off the mountaintop before you can grab it. Always pack your tent, fly, poles, and stakes in a handy spot in your backpack, boat, or vehicle. When the weather turns bad, you'll need to find

Chasm Lake, California

> While hiking, try to take constant note of prominent landmarks in relation to your surroundings. Keep comparing your surroundings to your map.

and set up your shelter quickly. Do what you can at home to make tent set-up easier in the field. Avoid tying knots in camp, especially when it's cold and you are wearing gloves. Tie permanent bowline knots at the ends of the guylines, so they can be easily slipped over the stakes. Keep zippers cleaned, lubricated, and running smoothly. Add zipper pulls. (See Zippers, Chapter 2.)

Learn how your portable stove operates. Practice assembling and lighting it at home. You will avoid stove flare-ups if you practice lighting and adjusting your stove. All stoves have idiosyncrasies; discover them at home, not in the field. Learn how to clean the stove. Keep your stove and pocketknife spotlessly clean.

Know Where You Are

While hiking, try to take constant note of prominent landmarks in relation to your surroundings. Keep comparing your surroundings to your map. If you become disoriented in the wilderness, your attitude is most important. Remain calm. Sit down. Eat a snack and drink some water. Then check your map and compass, and look around carefully. (See Maps and Compass, Chapter 2.) You may be able to recall where you took a wrong turn. Some signs that you may be lost include: a trail that was very clear, then suddenly became faint; no signs of trail markings; or unexpected landmarks not shown on your topo map. We all have moments of inattention while outdoors. A brief bout of daydreaming may leave you temporarily off-course. When you have calmly assessed your whereabouts, you can try to relocate your camp or trail by making short forays out and back in different directions, like the spokes on a wheel, always returning to the place where you first realized you were lost. Walk in a straight line on your forays. If you don't see familiar landmarks, return and try another direction. Take your time. Move slowly.

Always carry the following items, even when taking a short walk away from camp.

- Map
- Whistle
- Compass
- Knife
- Waterproof match safe

Safeguard these essentials by attaching them to yourself, either around your neck on a lanyard or on a secured key chain.

Remain Flexible

Be willing to change your route or even your overall plans. When you observe avalanche conditions while ski touring, when the dirt road deteriorates during a drive to a remote campground, when you see dark towers of clouds moving in fast when you're about to launch your boat, when you're hiking off-trail and your intended route appears too rugged for your equipment and abilities, confer with your companions. Be conservative. Alter your plans. You will still have a wonderful trip, just a slightly different one.

The Versatile Three

Tuck these three tiny, lightweight pieces of equipment into your camping box. They have dozens of uses.

- *Bandana.* You can use it for sun, rain, and insect protection for your face, head, and neck; as a washcloth; towel; sweatband; pot holder; preliminary water filter; and compress, to name a few.

- *Dental floss.* This versatile piece of equipment can be used as a clothesline (string it lengthwise inside your tent for drying and airing clothes and suspending gear out of the way), spare shoelace, sewing thread, or fishing line.

- *Nylon net.* You can adapt this to use it as a strainer for pasta or vegetables, plate and pot scrubber, bug net (drape over your hat and tuck it into your collar). Nylon net is available in fabric stores by the yard in fine or medium mesh. Use fine mesh as a bug net, medium mesh as a strainer or scrubber.

> Tuck a bandana, dental floss, and a nylon net into your camping box—three lightweight pieces of equipment that have dozens of uses.

Beyond No-Trace Camping

With so many of us using the wilderness, we must make every effort to leave the outdoors not only without evidence of our being there, but in a better, more natural condition than we found it. Take good care of our public lands and feel good about your efforts. Remove unsightly messes left by others, and leave clean camps for the next users. If you are backpacking above an elevation of 10,000 feet in an area where wood fires are now illegal, take some time to dismantle old fire rings as you encounter them. (See Campfires, Chapter 2, for fire ring cleanup suggestions.) Pick up trash whenever you find it. When you are car camping in a public campground, take a garbage bag with you as you walk around the campground's roads and trails. When you're backpacking, fasten a garbage bag to the outside of your pack to make litter pickup easy. When you're paddling, put lake or river refuse on board your boat and haul it out. If the pit privy at a remote public campground is lacking toilet paper, leave one of your extra rolls of toilet paper for the next camper.

Debriefing

After each trip, take a few minutes to make equipment notes. What gear that you took on this trip was not used? What did you not take that you really want to carry next time? Look at what you unpack with a critical eye. Was the sweater you took too bulky and heavy? If you write it down, you'll remember next time.

Analyze your trip overall. Did you spend too much time driving? Was August an overcrowded month at your destination? Would you like to carry some extra gallons of water in your vehicle next time? A few minutes of honest analysis now will make your next trip nearly perfect. Keep the dated notes in your travel file or as an afterword in your journal. For example:

2-week car camp trip, Adirondacks
September 1998

weather	warm days, cool nights, mainly dry
need	2 extra c-cell batteries (took 4, need 6)
did not use	mosquito head net, extra blanket, down vests

While unpacking your equipment, take time during the next few days to clean, repair, or replace gear, if needed. As you store your well-cared-for gear in your equipment boxes, enjoy your camping memories. Look at your maps and begin to plan your next trip. You're ready to go camping again as soon as you'd like.

2

BACKPACK IN
COMFORT

---

*They were struggling up the rocky, exposed pass. We saw them
and stopped to chat. His face was purple from the exertion
and his stomach wobbled over the waistband of his overstuffed pack. She could only nod, too breathless to speak. Their
narrow hat brims didn't protect their faces from the hot midday sun.*

*Perhaps they'd like to camp nearby? We pointed out a
bivouac site near a waterfall partway up the pass. "No," he
wheezed, "we're going on. We'll camp at Bench Lake tonight."
He'd studied the topo map. The distance over the pass and on
to the lake didn't appear to be many miles. He hadn't con-
sidered that in most mountain situations mileage is mean-
ingless. These backpackers were overloaded and unprepared
for this rugged route.*

More than most other sports, backpacking demands thoughtful
planning.

- Choose your equipment from the Backpack List found in this chapter.
- Take exactly the gear you need, no more.
- Learn everything you can about your chosen area.
- Study guidebooks and topo maps.
- Talk to rangers and experienced backpackers.
- Consider points of interest and difficulties of terrain, then pick a route that you will enjoy.

Paring down weight and setting a realistic pace and destination will make backpacking a pleasure.

Base Camp Bliss

During ambitious wilderness trips, you might find yourself a three-days' walk away from any trailhead. Here you will find solitude. But you don't need to hike that far to find a quiet campsite; you just need to explore. The right spot awaits your discovery.

Try a short-distance backpack trip. One day of easy, slow progress can take you a few miles into the backcountry. When you reach an area that seems likely for good camping and interesting day trips, cache your backpack out of sight. Explore the immediate area while carrying only your map, water, compass, and other essentials in your daypack. Look for a secluded campsite located off the trail at least 200 feet from a water source, with a gently sloping clearing to pitch your tent.

Camp for several nights in the same spot. Take day trips away from your base camp carrying only your map, compass, lunch, water, rain jacket, first aid, and emergency gear. Day outings can be relaxing or strenuous. They can include trail hiking, cross-country exploring, nature strolls, peak climbs, swimming, fishing, photography, writing, drawing, or daydreaming. For example, spend the day climbing a peak and photographing the views. Enjoy lunch on top of the mountain. At the end of the day, return to your already-set-up camp. Cook dinner on your portable stove; avoid building campfires in pristine locations. If you are an experienced backpacker used to long-distance trips, try a base camp trip as a "vacation." You may make a habit of it, or at least include a few refreshing days at a base camp partway through a long trek.

Paring Down

Your backpack, fully loaded, should not exceed one-third of your body weight. Be ruthless. Weigh yourself at home wearing your loaded pack and filled water containers. If you are over your weight limit, pare down now, before you leave. Most warm-weather backpack trips require little clothing. Shirt, socks, and underpants can be washed and air-dried during all but the worst weather. Washing your clothing in camp is a simple chore that also cleans your hands. Wear several very thin, lightweight layers of clothing, such as a light jacket and lightweight synthetic or silk long underwear. These lightweight layers dry quickly. They are warmer, lighter, and less bulky than single, heavy layers of clothing, such as a sweat suit. The air trapped between the lightweight layers serves as weightless insulation. Thin layers provide comfortable flexibility in any temperature.

> **Your fully loaded backpack should not exceed one-third of your body weight.**

Heavy canned food, fresh food, cooking oil, frying pans, extra pots, forks, mess kits, spatulas, cutting boards, and graters are best left at home or in the vehicle for car camping. Backpack with ready-to-heat, lightweight dried meals. (See Home-Dried One-Pot Meals, Chapter 1 or the menu plan and recipes below.)

Pack for Comfort

Your pack will feel lighter and more comfortable when you carry the weight high and close to your body and pack soft items against your back. Carry lightweight, bulky items at the bottom of your pack. Place heavy items high and close to your back. Try to keep the left and right sides of your pack equal in weight. Each morning before you break camp and hit the trail, put that day's snacks and water container within easy reach, then stow the rest of your food deep inside the pack. Keep your rain jacket, ground cloth, and tent handy

fully loaded backpack

near the top of the pack in case the weather suddenly deteriorates. Once you've found a good place in your pack for each item, repack the same way year after year. Flag the outside pack pockets with identifying colored ribbons such as red for first aid and blue for the water filter.

Getting and Staying in Shape

> **Flag the outside pack pockets with identifying colored ribbons such as red for first aid and blue for the water filter.**

It's sometimes easier to run a marathon than to carry a heavy backpack at high altitude over rough terrain. Backpacking is strenuous. If you exercise regularly, backpacking becomes far easier. Cycling, jogging, cross-country skiing, lifting weights, strengthening your abdominal muscles, and regular hiking will keep you feeling great year-round. Check with your physician and choose a fitness program that's right for you. Engage in some form of exercise daily, or at least three times a week. Vary your routine. Keep limber; include stretching in your exercise program. Don't choose partners for backpack trips until you have taken lengthy day hikes with them. Involve your camping partners in your exercise program so you will all be equally fit for upcoming trips.

Borrow, Rent, or Buy Equipment

Sleeping outdoors under the stars is more fun than sleeping in a tent, if the weather is good and it's not too buggy. If you're going into country where rain, snow, or clouds of insects are a distinct possibility, a lightweight tent will make your backpack trip far more comfortable and may save your life. It's ideal to have a good,

tent

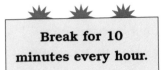

Break for 10 minutes every hour.

lightweight tent available when you need it. Another shelter choice is a bivy sack, a waterproof, breathable sack that slips over your sleeping bag and protects your face with a net; in decent weather it is an adequate, very lightweight shelter. If you're not ready to buy a quality backpack tent, rent or borrow one. Renting is a great opportunity to try before you buy. Backpacks, tents, sleeping bags, portable stoves, and even child carriers can be rented at surprisingly low cost. After you have tried rented or borrowed equipment on a few backpack trips, you will be a knowledgeable buyer. Buy only top-quality, lightweight equipment.

Pacing

The two young German backpackers passed us, moving fast. We hiked along at our usual gait, a slow, rolling, steady backpack pace. A few hours later, we passed the same backpackers as they sprawled, exhausted, beneath a tree. You may appear to be moving slowly, but a gentle pace will take you farther, and leave you less tired, than an uneven rush-then-collapse style.

✳　✳　✳

Hourly Breaks

Six to eight hours on the trail is ideal for most backpackers. Once in a while, a day of hiking unavoidably stretches out to 10 or 12 hours. You may become tired, but you will be able to hike as long as you need

Take hourly breaks.

to if you break for 10 minutes every hour. During a 10-minute break, you will rid your body of much of its lactic acid buildup. A break much longer than 10 minutes lets your body cool down too much, causing your muscles to stiffen. Stop religiously once an hour. Keep an eye on your wristwatch for accuracy. When you stop for a break, get your pack off your back. Take off and shake out your boots and socks. Elevate your feet. Let your body completely relax. Drink water. If you feel chilled while you are resting, put on your handy rain jacket.

The Rest Step

Take a break—while you're hiking. Practice resting one leg with each step. Just after your weight is transferred to your lead leg, let your rear leg relax completely, just for a fraction of a second, before lifting it. The rest step will help tired legs revive instantly.

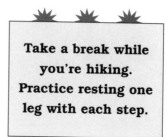

Take a break while you're hiking. Practice resting one leg with each step.

Sleep at High Elevation Before You Pack In

Give your body a chance to become adjusted to the lack of oxygen at high elevations. Become acclimated the easy way: overnight, while you are sleeping. If there are several campgrounds near your trailhead, choose the one located at the highest elevation. Overnight acclimation will help prevent mountain sickness, and simply makes a big difference in the way you feel. If you need to begin your backpack trip the same day you drive to the area, plan to pack in only a short distance, set up camp, and go to sleep early. Take it easy.

Prevent Acute Mountain Sickness

- Read Avoid Dehydration and Heatstroke in Chapter 1.
- Drink extra fluids.
- Snack constantly on carbohydrates.
- Take aspirin if needed for headaches. If your headache continues and you feel slight nausea and weakness, stop and camp. If you continue to feel ill, descend and camp at a lower elevation.
- Hike out if necessary.

At elevations above the 12,000 feet, High Altitude Pulmonary Edema or High Altitude Cerebral Edema, both potentially fatal, can occur. Symptoms include coughing, disorientation, severe headache, vomiting, and hallucinations. If any of these signs are present, descend immediately and seek emergency medical attention.

Know Where You Are

- Study your topo maps. (See Maps, this chapter.)
- Read guidebooks for recommended routes.
- Learn to orient using maps and compass. Then get off the trail a bit and explore if off-trail travel is permitted. Simply climbing to a viewpoint 200 feet off the trail will change your perspective.
- Memorize landmarks.
- Keep a tiny pad of paper and a pencil handy in your pocket. Draw yourself a map before you leave the trail. The act of observing, then drawing, will make you look carefully at your surroundings and help you relocate the trail if you get

turned around. Notes, used in conjunction with your compass and watch, will help you return to your camp. For example, if you've noted that you have hiked north from your camp for 45 minutes, then turned east and hiked 45 minutes longer, your point of origin lies roughly one hour's hike to the southwest.

Consider exploring a short cross-country section on backpack trips if off-trail travel is permitted and if the terrain is open, not too overgrown or fragile. No trail is as interesting as your own explorations.

Wilderness Permits

Plan ahead for your backcountry trip. Research the national park, wilderness area, or other region you'd like to visit. Check guidebooks and the Internet. Once you've chosen an area, obtain and study maps. Maps let you enjoy your trip three times: planning prior to your vacation, orienting in the wilderness, and reliving the trip afterward. (See Know Where You Are, and Maps, this chapter.)

A wilderness permit may be needed, so plan ahead. Permits are issued by the agency that oversees the area where you will enter the wilderness. A backpack trip that starts at a trailhead in a United States Forest Service Wilderness Area and continues into an adjacent National Park will require only a permit from the appropriate forest service district.

Call or write the park service or forest service that administers your chosen area. Request a wilderness permit application. The agencies that govern our public lands can answer your questions and they will send you information that will aid you as you plan your trip. They will help you avoid the most heavily used trails, and the times of greatest use, in their jurisdictions. Popular areas now use a quota system, limiting the number of users per day. The quota system greatly lessens crowds at popular trailheads and backcountry campsites. If a permit is not required, register with the local agency or sign the trailhead self-registration log for your own protection.

When you apply for your wilderness permit ahead of time, your trip will begin in a less stressful fashion. You will eliminate waiting in line at a ranger station, wasting much of the first morning of your backpack trip. Even more important, a reservation made ahead of time assures your use of the particular area, trails, or even popular wilderness campsites on the days you have chosen. You could be denied access to your area if you have not planned ahead.

If your chosen route involves a loop that takes you into the wilderness at one trailhead and out of the wilderness at another trailhead many miles away, arrange for a shuttle bus pickup or drive to the area in two vehicles, leaving one at each trailhead. Plan ahead. Arrangements must be in place before you pack into the wilderness.

wilderness permit application

Itinerary

Leave your itinerary with a trusted friend or relative at home. Make a copy of your topo map and highlight your route. Mark your likely campsites. Give your friend the phone number of the ranger station nearest to your destination and a description of your vehicle, including the license plate number. Tell your friend if he or she

> **Leave your itinerary with a trusted friend or relative at home.**

hasn't seen you or received a phone call from you by a set date and time to call the ranger and give your vehicle description and itinerary. Then be sure when you get out of the wilderness to call your friend before the appointed date and time. An unnecessary search could be costly in time, money, and, most important, the safety of your rescuers. Always carry your friend's phone number and coins or a phone card.

Zippers

To make zippers easier to grip in gloved hands and in the dark, tie a few inches of cord or attach metal, rubber, or plastic rings to all your zipper tabs.

zipper pulls

Zippers run more smoothly when lubricated. Brush them with silicone lubricant, available from camping stores, or rub zippers lightly with a bar of hard soap. Failed zippers can often be repaired by pinching or replacing the slider. In most cases, zippers are easier to repair than to remove and replace. Repair kits for both light and heavyweight zippers are available at camping stores.

> **Zippers run more smoothly when lubricated. Rub zippers lightly with a bar of hard soap.**

Water Containers

Sturdy plastic water containers are lightweight and will last for years. Metal water containers are noisy and may dent if they are dropped or scraped against rock. Take one or two canteens per person in one-quart or one-liter sizes. Each person needs a canteen holder that will keep one water-filled canteen within reach on the trail.

In addition to individual canteens, take a large collapsible plastic water container. These are available in 1½-, 2½-, or 5-gallon sizes. The 5-gallon size would only be needed by a large group, and its weight when filled may require two people to carry it. A group-sized water container makes it easy to haul water from stream to campsite, and the container can be set in the sun to heat water for washing people, clothes, and dishes.

plastic canteen

Backpack List Details

Backpack: Borrow, rent, or buy one that feels comfortable. Fill it with weights before trying it on. Look for a pack with a well-padded waist belt and shoulder straps. Pin large safety or diaper pins to the edges of your pack for hanging wet laundry. You can waterproof the whole main compartment by lining it with a heavy plastic bag, or individually bag your gear in sturdy plastic bags. No backpack is completely waterproof.

Daypack: Take a lightweight daypack for day hikes away from your camp. Choose one just large enough to carry lunch, water, rain jacket, first aid, and emergency gear. Use your daypack as an organizer inside your backpack to keep important personal items together.

Tent: Borrow, rent, or buy a three-season tent for most uses, or a four-season tent for winter camping. Keep your tent clean and protect it from tears and punctures. Reseal the seams with seam sealant every few years.

Sleeping Bag: Goose down is the lightest and warmest fill, but

BACKPACK LIST

This is the master list for preparing for a backpack trip. The backpack list details include some of the list items and tips on how to choose and care for your camping gear.

Shelter

- ❏ Backpack
- ❏ Daypack
- ❏ Tent
  - ❏ Fly
  - ❏ Poles
  - ❏ Stakes + 2 extra
- ❏ Sleeping bag
  - ❏ Stuff sacks
- ❏ Sleeping pad
- ❏ Ground cloth
- ❏ Extra plastic bags
- ❏ 50-foot nylon cord

Clothing

- ❏ Boots
  - ❏ Insoles
- ❏ Brimmed hat
- ❏ Glacier glasses
- ❏ Knit cap
- ❏ Mosquito head net
- ❏ Waterproof jacket and pants
- ❏ Deerskin gloves
- ❏ Lightweight synthetic gloves
- ❏ Bandana
- ❏ Gaiters
- ❏ Sweater
- ❏ Trousers
- ❏ Nylon belt
- ❏ Belt pack
- ❏ 3 pairs heavy socks
- ❏ 3 pairs liner socks
- ❏ Long-sleeved shirt
- ❏ 2 T-shirts
- ❏ 2 pairs underpants
- ❏ Nylon shorts
- ❏ Synthetic long underwear
- ❏ Camp slippers or athletic shoes

Safety and Route Finding

- ❏ Whistle
- ❏ Flashlight
  - ❏ Extra batteries

BACKPACK LIST (CONTINUED)

- ☐ Matches and match safe
- ☐ Paper
- ☐ Pen
- ☐ Pencil
- ☐ Wristwatch
- ☐ Pocketknife
- ☐ Compass
- ☐ Maps
- ☐ Compact binoculars
- ☐ Phone numbers and addresses
- ☐ Wilderness permit reservation
- ☐ Credit card and cash, including coins

Toiletries

- ☐ Toilet paper
- ☐ Comb
- ☐ Sunscreen
- ☐ Tube of petroleum jelly
- ☐ Aloe vera cream
- ☐ Lip balm with sunscreen
- ☐ Insect repellent
- ☐ Benzocaine
- ☐ Premoistened wipes

- ☐ Packable viscose towel
- ☐ Toothbrush
- ☐ Toothpaste
- ☐ Dental floss
- ☐ Toothpicks
- ☐ Multivitamins
- ☐ Personal medications

First Aid

- ☐ Bandages
- ☐ Gauze pads
- ☐ Elastic bandage
- ☐ Tweezers
- ☐ Aspirin
- ☐ Antihistamine
- ☐ Bismuth tablets
- ☐ Salt
- ☐ Baking soda

Repair Kit

- ☐ 2 needles
- ☐ Thread
- ☐ Rip-stop tape
- ☐ Safety pins
- ☐ Rubber bands

BACKPACK LIST (CONTINUED)

- ❏ Extra flashlight bulb
- ❏ Metal rings for packs
- ❏ Fishing line and hooks
- ❏ Tent pole repair sleeve
- ❏ Crampon key
  (if needed)

Foot Kit

- ❏ 2nd Skin
- ❏ Moleskin
- ❏ New-Skin liquid
  bandage
- ❏ Rubbing alcohol
- ❏ Scissors
- ❏ Micropore tape
- ❏ Lamb's wool
- ❏ Bandages
- ❏ Needle
- ❏ Matches
- ❏ Nail clippers

Food and Water

- ❏ Water filter or
  purification tablets
- ❏ Canteens, 1 or 2 per
  person

- ❏ Belt holder
- ❏ Collapsible water jug
- ❏ Aluminum pot and lid
- ❏ Sierra cup
- ❏ Aluminum teaspoon
- ❏ Portable stove
- ❏ Full container of fuel
- ❏ Liquid soap
- ❏ Nylon net
- ❏ Sponge
- ❏ Salt

Personal

- ❏ Keys, house and vehicle
- ❏ Camera
  - ❏ Extra film
- ❏ Books to read
- ❏ Nature guides

Mountaineering Gear

- ❏ Ice axe with wrist leash
- ❏ Instep crampons
  - ❏ Crampon key (in
    repair kit)
- ❏ 50-foot climbing rope

it is useless when wet. Synthetic fill is excellent in wet conditions, although it is heavier, bulkier, and not as warm as down. Keep your sleeping bag dry and protected from abrasion. (See Bag It, Chapter 1, for the safest method.) Wash your sleeping bag as infrequently as possible. Spot-clean it, then air dry it after each trip. When you must wash your sleeping bag, do so carefully, by hand, on a warm, breezy day. Fluff and shift the fill while drying the bag as quickly and gently as possible.

Sleeping Pads: Closed-cell foam pads are lightweight and shed water. Hip length-size pads (also known as ¾ length) roll up compactly. Air mattresses are heavier and bulkier but more luxurious. Pad the inside of your sleeping bag with your bundled up clothes to avoid carrying the weight of a sleeping pad on warm-weather, ultralight trips.

Ground Cloth: Protects tent, sleeping bag, sleeping pad, and you from rain, snow, dirt, and rocks. A sheet of 3-mil polyethylene will last for years; it can be bought inexpensively by the foot in hardware supply stores. Coated nylon ground cloths are very light and flexible. Canvas cloths are too heavy. A grommeted ground cloth (tarp) can double as a lean-to shelter. A second ground cloth placed inside your tent will keep you dry and warm during heavy rain or on snow. (See Sleep Comfortably, Chapter 1.)

Extra Plastic Bags: Cover packs during wet weather with large-sized plastic trash bags slit up the right and left sides of the back to accommodate pack straps; secure the plastic bag with rubber bands or nylon cord. A large bag can also serve as an emergency rain poncho, after poking a hole in the bag for your face. An extra supply of medium- and small-sized plastic bags replaces other bags that become worn and holds your own and others' garbage while you pack it out. An extra garbage bag fastened to the outside of your pack will make it convenient to pick up and pack out litter wherever you find it.

50-foot nylon cord: Use to counterbalance food to protect it from bears. (See Counterbalance Food, Chapter 1.) Lash gear to pack. Hang as a clothesline, or make an emergency lean-to shelter from a grommeted ground cloth (tarp).

Boots: Get the best you can afford. Boots are your most important piece of equipment. To get the best fit, buy boots or any footwear during the afternoon; feet swell during the day. Wear two pairs of socks, heavy outer socks and thin liner socks, plus extra insoles—if you like additional cushioning—when you try on boots. Break in new boots before you hike. Fill them with warm water and let them stand for a few minutes. Drain the boots, then wear them at home, along with two pairs of socks, until they are dry. Take care of your boots and they will last for many years. Clean and waterproof them with wax-based waterproofing, or the type of waterproofing recommended by the manufacturer, between trips. Don't dry wet boots by a fire, a heater, in the sun, or inside the hot trunk of a car.

Brimmed Hat: Wear the widest brim you can find in a packable cotton or nylon hat. Add an elastic chin strap if your hat does not have a drawcord.

Glacier Glasses: Dark sunglasses with side shields protect your eyes from glare and wind. (See Protect Your Skin and Eyes, Chapter 1.)

Knit Cap: Synthetic dries faster than wool.

Mosquito Head Net: Must be worn over a brimmed hat to keep netting—and bugs—away from your face. Available at camping stores, or sew one yourself; no seeum nylon net fabric is available by mail from Campmor; call (800) 525-4784 for information.

Waterproof Jacket and Pants: Essential for wet or windy weather or as emergency clothing when your other clothes are wet.

Deerskin Gloves: Protect hands and allow enough sensitivity for rock climbing. Deerskin remains flexible and soft even when wet.

Lightweight Synthetic Gloves: Can be worn alone or layered under heavy gloves or mittens.

Bandana: Use cotton bandanas as head, neck, or face protectors in sun or cold weather, or as a compress, washcloth, or towel.

Gaiters: Nylon, medium weight, when needed for snow, or heavy brush off-trail.

Sweater: Take one that's lightweight and warm, made of wool or synthetic fabric.

Trousers: Cotton or nylon if warm, wool if cold. Only one pair is needed for most backpack trips; shorts, rain pants, or long underwear can be temporarily substituted if trousers get soaked.

Nylon Belt: A nylon web belt is strong, stable, and sheds water, unlike leather.

Belt Pack: Small nylon pack slides onto belt for frequently used small items such as compass, matches in match safe, whistle, pocketknife, lip balm, and sunscreen.

nylon belt pack

Heavy Socks: Choose wool, synthetic, or a combination of these fabrics for good cushioning. Avoid cotton, which can bunch and cause blisters and is slow to dry.

Liner Socks: Prevent blisters and wick moisture away from your feet. Silk, nylon, or polyester are good choices. Cotton tends to ruck and cause blisters.

Long-Sleeved Shirt: For protection from sun and wind. Choose light-colored, loose-fitting cotton with snap, zipper, Velcro, or button-closed pockets.

T-shirts: Synthetic fabric wicks away moisture better than cotton.

Underpants: Take lightweight, comfortable, quick-drying underwear.

Nylon Shorts: Choose lightweight, fast-drying shorts, such as running shorts. They can double as underpants or as a bathing suit.

Synthetic Long Underwear: Should be included on almost every trip. Take a complete set, including a zip-front turtleneck, a pair of long johns, a knit cap, socks, and gloves. Silk, polyester, or polypropylene, unlike cotton, wick perspiration away from your body to keep you warm and comfortable. They are also less bulky, lighter, and dry more quickly.

Camp Slippers: Ease your feet when you stop for the day—put on clean socks and camp slippers. Shop at a discount store for the lightest-weight hard-soled house slippers you can find. The least expensive slippers are often the lightest in weight. Very lightweight athletic shoes are another good choice; they are sturdier but heavier than slippers.

Whistle: Must be loud. Use in emergencies only, or to signal other members of your party. One blast of the whistle indicates your whereabouts. Three successive blasts are the universal call for help.

complete set of synthetic long underwear

Flashlight and Extra Batteries: Stretch a thick rubber band or a piece of duct tape over the flashlight's switch to keep from accidentally turning it on and draining the batteries. Load your flashlights with fresh batteries prior to your trip. Take at least one set of extra, fresh batteries for each flashlight. Use the length of your trip and your personal needs to estimate

camp slippers

how many hours of light you'll need. (Chris, an avid backpacker, insists on reading late into the night. He carries dozens of extra flashlight batteries on every backpack trip and says that for him the considerable extra weight is justified.)

> **Three successive whistle blasts are the universal call for help.**

Matches and Match Safe: Take at least one pack per day per person. Store them in plastic bags in various locations in your shirt and jacket pockets and in your daypack and backpack. Keep some waterproof, windproof matches dry in a match safe.

Paper, Pen, and Pencil: Keep a journal, draw, write messages. Use the paper, or bills from your wallet, to start an emergency campfire.

Wristwatch: Keep track of breaks, hours of daylight remaining, and the hiking time to your destination, so you can estimate the amount of time needed to return. Coordinate meetings with the rest of your party.

Pocketknife: Choose a good-quality folding pocketknife or multifunction camper's tool. Consider your needs—and the weight and effectiveness of the knife—when choosing the number of featured tools. The knife's most vital tool is a sharp blade: it will help you create kindling for an emergency campfire. Handle your knife with care and respect. Keep it clean and handy in a belt pouch; don't set it down or carry it loose in a pocket.

Compass: Learn how to orient yourself with your compass and never be without it.

Maps: Fold your topo map so the side you're using is facing out and protect it by storing it in a one-gallon zip-top bag.

Compact Binoculars: Choose the best cross-country routes, read the river, and view wildlife.

Phone Numbers and Addresses: For emergency calls.

Wilderness Permit Reservation: If required, obtain by mail from national park, forest service, or other agency before your trip.

Request a campfire permit as well to use either a backpack stove or a campfire.

Credit Card and Cash, Including Coins: Include coins or a phone card for telephone calls.

Toilet Paper: One roll per person lasts for a 10-day backpack trip, with plenty to spare. Store the roll in a plastic bag. Step on it to compact it.

Comb: Tiny travel or child-sized.

Sunscreen: Since you'll apply this liberally several times a day, keep it handy in a small, screw-top, bagged container. Flip-top lids can open and leak; if you use flip-top containers, tape them shut before you bag them.

Tube of Petroleum Jelly: Half a tube of the smallest travel size is plenty. Use for chafing, squeaky equipment, and tick removal. Lubricate your body and your equipment.

Aloe Vera Cream: Put a little in a tiny screw-top plastic container for sunburn, windburn, or itchy insect-bitten skin.

Lip Balm with Sunscreen: Choose one containing sunscreen and apply it often.

Insect Repellent: Keep handy in a screw-top plastic bottle. Apply it to clothing (hat brim, shirt cuffs, and collar) rather than skin.

Benzocaine: If you've ever been kept awake by itching insect bites, you'll want to pack a container of benzocaine. Several brands are available specifically for the treatment of insect bites.

Premoistened Wipes: Take several per day per person. They must be packed out, but are very lightweight.

Packable Viscose Towel: A small lightweight towel made of viscose dries very quickly. Alternatively, take a very thin, worn, cotton hand towel or use your bandana.

Toothbrush, Toothpaste, Dental Floss, and Toothpicks: Buy the smallest sizes you can find in the travel section of your drugstore.

Multivitamins: If desired, pack one per day and take with breakfast.

Personal Medications: Take a supply of prescription or other needed medications, including labels and directions, in plastic bags.

First Aid: Bandages and sterile gauze pads to protect cuts and scrapes, after cleaning them with soap and water. Elastic bandage for sprains, tweezers for splinter and tick removal. (Cover tick with petroleum jelly or rubbing alcohol, wait briefly, then pull out, being careful to remove entire tick). Aspirin for pain and swelling, antihistamine for insect bites, allergies, hives, colds, and most respiratory problems. Bismuth tablets for upset stomach, diarrhea, or nausea. Baking soda mixed with a small amount of water can be applied as a paste to bee stings and mosquito bites; it also serves as a throat-soothing gargle when ¼ teaspoon is dissolved with ¼ teaspoon salt in a cup of warm water, and its gentle abrasion can be used to clean teeth, cooking pots, or almost anything else. You may want to include for long, remote trips: splint, bite extractor, emergency dental kit, antibiotics, and an emergency wilderness medical guide.

> **Baking soda mixed with a small amount of water can be applied as a paste to bee stings and mosquito bites.**

Repair Kit: A one-foot length of nylon rip-stop tape, available at camping stores, can repair sleeping bag, jacket, and tent rips. Take a couple of spare metal rings to reconnect your pack to its external frame. If you break a tent pole, a five-inch-long piece of PVC or aluminum pipe of slightly larger diameter than the pole can slip over the pole; secure the pipe with tape.

Foot Kit: Keep handy for quick foot treatment at rest stops. 2nd Skin and moleskin can be secured, if needed, with micropore tape. Trim adhesive pads and cut tape with a tiny pair of children's blunt-end scissors if your pocketknife doesn't have scissors. Lamb's wool can pad sore spots on feet and ankles.

> **Never clean the outside of your aluminum pot; it will heat more evenly as it blackens.**

Water: Borrow or buy a good microporous filter, or boil all your drinking water for three minutes, or use iodine tablets. Never drink untreated water. Take one or two heavy-duty plastic canteens per person. Use a collapsible water jug as a communal water source. Placed in the sun, it can heat water for a backpack shower in base camp.

Pots and Utensils: One two-quart aluminum pot is sufficient for a party of two or three people, a three-quart pot for four people. Bring the lightest-weight pot you can find. It should be wide in diameter and low-sided for better balance. Never clean the outside of the pot; it will heat more evenly as it blackens. Store the pot in a heavy plastic bag. No forks are needed, just one spoon, pocketknife, and Sierra cup per person.

Backpack Stove and Fuel: Borrow, rent, or buy a reliable lightweight model.

Cleaning Supplies: Take a small amount of biodegradable liquid soap, a one-foot square of nylon net as a scrubber, a sponge for wiping rain off tent and other equipment, and a tablespoon of salt in a small plastic bag to use on food or as a cleanser or gargle.

Personal: Keep the keys to your house and vehicle fastened to you or attached to the inside of your pack. Protect camera and film from moisture; store in a heavy plastic bag. Take a paperback book that is absorbing enough to last through a storm.

Mountaineering: Let an experienced person teach you how to use an ice axe, instep crampons, and climbing rope. If you come across

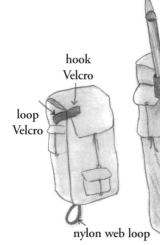

hook
Velcro

loop
Velcro

nylon web loop

Sew an ice axe holder to your backpack.

ice or snow fields, an ice axe may prevent injuries. A longer length ice axe that serves as a walking stick helps with rock scrambling and stream crossings. Add a wrist leash made of nylon webbing to your ice axe. Sew a Velcro holder and nylon web loop to your backpack to store axe when not in use.

Small instep crampons let you cross snowfields and glaciers quickly and safely. Climbing rope is heavy and expensive; learn how to use it, and carry it when safety dictates.

Maps

The snow started at dawn. We were bivouacked, without a tent, just below the pass. It was cold. In our hasty decision to drop altitude, we took a cross-country route, the quickest way down, according to the topo (topographic) map. We later learned that we'd chosen one of the worst cross-country routes in the Sierra Nevada mountains. We waded for endless hours in the swift, icy Kings River, and bushwhacked along the river's steep, aspen-tangled banks. A terrified bear crashed through the underbrush a few feet away from us. We were likely the first humans he had ever seen. Two days later we stumbled out of the canyon, having learned a valuable map-reading lesson: anticipate more difficulties than can be seen on a topo map.

✳　✳　✳

Detailed topo maps—in conjunction with your compass, good observation, research prior to your trip, and sound judgment—are your best guides. However, topo maps cannot reveal the depth or temperature of the rivers, the amount of snow, the difficulties posed by adverse weather conditions, the thickness of the vegetation, or the number of mosquitoes. More than once, we'd planned on camping at high alpine lakes, then found them locked in deep shade, snowbound and frozen solid—during the summer. A true understanding of the landscape and the all-important conditions at the time of your visit comes only when you arrive and explore the area.

Detailed road maps, available from commercial mapmakers, the forest service, or other governmental agencies, will help guide you to trailheads. You need these detailed road maps to negotiate back roads. Road maps are not adequate for hiking.

**The Muro Blanco,
California**

Rely on United States Geological Survey and Canadian National Topographic Series topographic maps for hiking. These are commonly called topo maps. *Topo maps* indicate the shape of the land. They do this by using brown contour lines to show altitude changes. Widely spaced contour lines indicate gentle topography. Closely spaced lines indicate steep terrain. The elevation distances between these lines are known as contour intervals. At the bottom of each topo map, note the contour interval for that individual map. Contour intervals can be anywhere from 10 to 100 feet; the difference in these intervals represents a great difference in the ruggedness of the terrain. If the map's contour interval is 100 feet and the brown contour lines are close together, the map is displaying an impassably steep land formation.

The green areas of topo maps show woodlands or other vegetation, white areas indicate little vegetation, and blue is used to show waterways or to outline glaciers or dry waterbeds. Topo maps display natural features: streams, rivers, valleys, and mountains. They also indicate human-made features: roads,

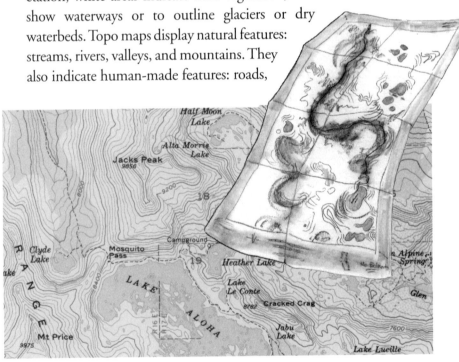

topo maps

trails, mines, dams, bridges, and other structures. Both the natural and especially the human-made features may be different now than they were when the topo map was created. Note the date of publication at the bottom of the map; some have not been updated since the 1950s. A few topo maps show trails that were constructed many years ago but have not been maintained. You can no longer call these log- and boulder-strewn cross-country routes trails. Always research trail and cross-country route conditions. Read guidebooks. Ask local rangers.

> **Some topo maps provided by the United States Geological Survey and Canadian National Topographic Series have not been updated since the 1950s and may not reflect changing terrain or features of an area.**

Buy topo maps prior to your trip. Topo maps are sold at camping, mining, and survey stores. If your local store doesn't have maps for the area you have chosen, ask them to order what you need. Or you can order your United States maps from the United States Department of the Interior Geological Survey on the Internet at http://www-nmd.usgs.gov/ or by telephone at (800) HELP-MAP, or by at fax (303) 202-4693. Order Canadian maps and river guides on the Internet at http://www.dogears.com/dog-ears.htm or contact them by E-mail at staff@dogears.com or write Dog Ears, Suite 327, 900 Greenbank Road, Ottawa, Ontario, K2J4P6, Canada. Choose one of the following sized topo map quadrangles:

- The 15-minute (197 to 282 square miles, less detailed) series is sufficient for most trail hiking. This size topo is popular and readily available. Just one map may display your entire route.

- The 7½-minute (49 to 70 square miles, more detailed) size is invaluable for cross-country travel, when you need all available information. You will often need more than one of these detailed maps to show your entire route.

Trim the margins off your maps. Align the maps to fit inside a one-gallon zip-top plastic bag. Fold the maps, with the section you need first showing, then seal them in the plastic bags.

Route Selection

Map study and route selection are some of the most exciting parts of your trip. Dream your way through several possible trips, then choose the most appealing route.

Loop trips and out-and-back trips make the logistics easy. You park your vehicle near the trailhead and return to it at the end of your backpack trip. If your entry and exit trailheads are some distance apart, you can sometimes arrange for a shuttle bus pickup.

Glacier Lake, Kings Canyon National Park, California

Other possible logistic choices for trailheads several miles apart are: take two vehicles and leave one at each trailhead, make the acquaintance of other campers and ask them for a ride, or walk back to your vehicle by road.

If your entry and exit trailheads are very far apart, try a vehicle exchange trip. We once left our vehicle on the eastern side of the Sierra Nevada, then spent 10 leisurely days hiking across to the western side of the range. Our partners did the trip in reverse. We met them mid-trip. After a night spent camping together in a remote, trail-less basin, we exchanged car keys, continued our respective backpack routes, and drove home in each others' vehicles.

Study guidebooks that detail trails and cross-country routes in the area you will visit. Consider the book's recommended routes. Pay attention to warnings about seasonal hazards. Carefully read descriptions of trail and cross-country routes. Routes described as "easy" or "moderate" are challenging enough for beginning or intermediate backpackers. Routes described vaguely as "a way may be found" are likely difficult, off-trail stretches for experienced mountaineers. If routes are numerically rated in the guidebooks, treat those ratings with respect. The difference between a Class 2 and a Class 3 route can be appreciable.

- Class 2 generally indicates walking without handholds, though the terrain may be steep.
- Class 3 might involve climbing, using handholds, and can be difficult when you are carrying a full backpack.

Look for the potentially difficult parts of your chosen trip on the topo map. Allow plenty of extra time to negotiate steep routes, river crossings, and any off-trail travel. A rugged quarter mile of cross-country travel could take two hours to negotiate. Remember to think in terms of hours and days, not miles. If you have rough terrain ahead of you, plan to cover very little distance that day. Discuss with all members of your party the locations of the nearest ranger stations and trailheads, and decide where you would exit the wilderness or seek help if needed. Look for the backcountry ranger stations shown on your topo map. When you obtain your wilderness permit, ask which of these ranger stations are staffed during the time of your visit.

    If you've been lucky and have never been lost, you may think you don't need a compass. Carry one at all times for safety, and also for the enjoyment brought by increased awareness of your surroundings. A compass will keep you on course

> **Compass**
>
> **"I'll just be hiking on trails, so I don't need to carry a compass."**
>
> **"I've been hiking my whole life. I don't need a compass because I have a good sense of direction."**

when you're making your way through a dense forest, when you're in terrain that has few landmarks, or when the landscape has been transformed by fog or snow. Simply checking your compass periodically will save you wasted time refinding your camp or trail, and could even save your life.

    As you leave your camp for a day hike, look at your compass. Note in which direction you are hiking toward your intended destination. Observe prominent landmarks in relation to your camp. You may decide to leave the trail to climb a peak. A thick fog could descend while you are still on the mountain. If you have checked your compass a few times that day, you will know where you are camped in relation to the peak. Your compass will show you the way down the mountain. Without a compass you could wander for hours, tired and hungry, in the fog.

    Don't wait until your next backpack trip to try orienting. Experiment with your compass close to home, using a local topo map. Align your map with your compass. Turn the map so it echoes the actual terrain, with north on the map matching north on your compass. Allow for east or west declination of your compass.

Declination means the degrees of difference between magnetic north, where the compass's needle is pointing, and actual geographic north at the top of the world. You will find the declination for your area noted on the bottom of each individual topo map. When locating north on your map and compass, allow for the degrees of declination shown on your topo map. Find some local landmarks on your map. Compare them with the landscape as you actually see it.

River Crossings

Respect all rivers; their currents may be stronger than they appear. Cross with the utmost caution. First, take some time to scout. If there are no human-made bridges in the vicinity, you'll need to cross on a large log, rocks that form a bridge or semi-bridge across the water, or by wading directly through the water. Unfasten your pack's waist belt before any river crossing, either in the water or across a log or rock bridge. If you slip, you may need to remove your pack quickly.

Look for a large, solid log to use as a bridge. You can choose to walk across it slowly, with your arms outstretched for balance. Logs across creeks and rivers are often slippery from lichen and dampness. Move carefully. If you feel nervous crossing on foot, don't be **compass** ashamed to straddle the log and scoot across the river on your bottom, bracing yourself with your hands and inching forward.

If you have no log or rock bridges, choose wide, shallow, gentle places to walk across the river, not swift and narrow ones. Yes, you'll be in the water longer, but you will have a better chance of getting safely to the other side. If you are crossing the river alone, support yourself with a walking stick, ice axe, or sturdy branch.

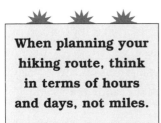

Wedge the stick firmly ahead of you on your upstream side before each step. Lean upstream against the current. A group of people negotiating a deep, swift creek or river should cross together. The party can combine their weight and strength by linking arms, grasping the same pole or dead tree limb, or holding rope that has been secured to a boulder. When wading through the water, wear your boots, rather than go barefoot. Sharp rocks, sticks, and hidden debris could cut or puncture your feet. If your trip requires many river crossings, bring a pair of nylon athletic shoes and a pair of nylon shorts. Tie them to the outside of your pack and use them for river crossings.

To arrive on the other bank of the river with fairly dry clothing, first remove your boots and socks. If you're wearing trousers rather than shorts, take off your trousers and pack them, along with your socks, inside your backpack. Put on your boots, securely laced, minus the socks. When you reach the other side of the river, drain your boots for a few minutes, dry your feet and legs, then replace your trousers, socks, and boots.

Backpack Campsites

Gorgeous vistas, dramatic sunsets, and sunrises enjoyed from a high mountain perch can be the highlights of your backpack trip. Before your trip, study the topo maps to find intriguing spots to spend the night. Circle possible campsites and alternate campsites with a pencil. When you arrive at a potential camp-

> **When planning your hiking route, think in terms of hours and days, not miles.**

> **When in wooded areas, look up before you camp. Don't set up your sleeping, eating, or cooking area underneath dead or dying trees or limbs or loose boulders that could fall on you.**

site, take off your pack and walk around. Sit down and consider. Would you like to live in this location for one or more evenings? Some campers prefer very open, high areas with terrific views and are willing to do without sheltering trees in all but the windiest weather. Others feel more comfortable in a cozier setting, surrounded by trees and protected by boulders.

Certain basics most of us hope to find at backcountry campsites are:

- A level, slightly sloping, well-drained area on which to sleep
- A good water source nearby
- Some shelter from high winds and weather

If you are in a heavily used area, use an existing campsite. If you choose a pristine location, take great care not to disturb it. When you can, make camp on gravel or mineral soil rather than disturb fragile soil and plants. Don't build a wood fire; use a portable stove. As soon as you have chosen your camp, take off your boots. Put on dry socks and camp slippers. Slippers are far less disturbing to the soil than lug-soled boots. Avoid campsites on the shores of lakes. Set up camp at least 200 feet away from any watercourse or any gully that could turn into a watercourse overnight. If you must move rocks or logs in order to squeeze your tent into a small area, replace them and naturalize the area when you break camp. (See Sleep Comfortably, Chapter 1, for maximizing comfort and minimizing impact when you set up your tent.)

When in wooded areas, look up before you camp. Don't set up your sleeping, eating, or cooking area underneath dead or dying trees or limbs or loose boulders that could fall on you. If you choose to camp on a scenic ledge overlooking a thousand-foot drop, use caution. Turn on your flashlight as soon as you get up in the middle of the night.

Beyond these basic requirements for comfort and safety, we all have deeper needs. Some places are special due to their remoteness, great beauty, huge views, or abundant wildlife. You may be willing to walk a little distance to your water source if you find a very special location in which to camp. Balance environmental and safety concerns with aesthetic needs.

Packing with Your Dog

Can you and your outdoors-loving dog enjoy a wilderness trip together? Yes, but only if domestic animals are permitted in your chosen backcountry area, if your pet is physically able, and if you have good control of your dog at all times. Domestic animals are not permitted or welcomed in many wilderness settings, so first

**Mt. Shasta from the
Trinity Alps, California**

learn the rules. If welcome, your dog will need a leash and an identification tag. Keep it on the leash when it's carrying its pack (see below). Keep it close to you and quiet at all times, and don't let it worry wildlife or people.

Let your large- or medium-sized dog carry its own pack. Buy or sew a well-balanced, waterproofed nylon pack. It must strap on comfortably and securely around the dog's chest and undersides. Nylon webbing straps, with plastic snap-shut buckles, are the easiest pack fasteners to put on, adjust, and remove. Necessity or desire will take your dog into the water, so waterproof food and equipment by double-bagging everything in heavy plastic before putting it inside the dog's pack (see Keep Gear Dry, Chapter 5).

Commercial dog packs have grommeted water drain holes in their bottoms. If you decide to make a dog pack, add a few reinforced drain holes along the bottom. Load the pack with dog food, a container of water, if necessary, and a few pieces of unbreakable gear, such as a small cooking pot. Take time to balance the left and right sides of the pack. If you aren't able to make them equal, put a small, unbreakable object from your own pack into the lighter weight side of the dog's pack. If your dog has tender paws, consider dog booties if you will be traveling over sharp rocks or very hot surfaces.

> **Don't let your animal become dehydrated. Keep your dog happy with plenty of food and water. It will be easier to control if it's comfortable.**

Don't let your animal become dehydrated. Study your route carefully for accessible water stops. If water is infrequently available, you must carry water for your dog or let it carry its own. Take a lightweight, collapsible water dish.

Clean up your dog's waste, especially near any trail or campsite. Pack out dog feces or bury them in the same responsible way you bury your own (see Human Waste Disposal, Chapter 1).

Trail Laundry

Scoop water into your clean cooking pot, large group water container, or collapsible bucket and walk 200 feet away from any water source. When weather permits, wash your clothes. Using just a drop of biodegradable soap, or no soap at all, wash your socks, bandana, underpants, and shirt. Wring the washed clothing thoroughly, then spread it on rocks and be sure to weight down each piece of clothing with good-sized rocks. When the wind picks up, your unweighted laundry could blow over to the next mountain ridge. If your clothes are still damp by nightfall, hang them inside your tent on a clothesline made of dental floss.

Don't be concerned if your clothes are not completely dry in the morning. You can use your backpack as a clothesline. Before you leave home, pin large safety or diaper pins on all the

Dry laundry on your backpack.

zipper tabs and around the hems of your backpack. While on the trail, pin your damp clothes to your pack—they will flap dry as you walk.

Keep Days Short

Stop early. Try to camp just before you plan to climb a difficult pass, a steep stretch of trail, or a slow cross-country route. If possible, end your day of hiking at 3 or 4 P.M. As soon as you stop to camp, take off your hiking boots. Put on clean, dry socks and your comfortable camp slippers or lightweight athletic shoes. Do a little laundry, take some photographs, identify the local flora and fauna, or write in your journal. Relax and enjoy the late afternoon and evening. Then get up early the next morning and cross the pass while you are fresh and the day is cool. Six to eight hours on the trail is ideal.

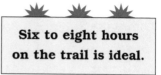

Six to eight hours on the trail is ideal.

The Magical Third Day

At the beginning of each camping trip, your backpack may feel impossibly heavy. You might feel restless for the first night or two. Routines while living outdoors seem to require more thought and effort than, for example, turning on the hot water faucet or switching on the electric light at home.

On every trip, you wake up on the morning of your third day out and feel absolutely wonderful.

But somehow, on every trip, you wake up on the morning of your third day out and feel absolutely wonderful. You have completely adjusted to the thinner air in the mountains after sleeping at high altitude for two nights. Living outdoors seems easy and natural. Your pack doesn't feel nearly as heavy. You could live this way forever.

Backpacker's Shower

While staying in base camp, fill a solar shower bag or a collapsible clear plastic jug with water. Set it on a rock in full sun in the morning. You will have warm shower water by afternoon.

When you're moving to a new campsite each night and don't have enough hours in camp to heat water using the sun, or if the weather is overcast, use your portable stove to heat water. One potful of warm water will clean one person.

Wash yourself at least 200 feet away from any camp or water source. Strip, then pour a little water over your head. Using the smallest amount of biodegradable soap possible, wash your hair, then scrub and rinse the rest of your body. Use your bandana as a washcloth. Dry yourself using a viscose towel, or use another bandana or any piece of quick-drying clothing.

Campfires

In some wilderness situations, an open campfire is truly necessary to warm and dry people and gear, but a campfire is often a dirty, dangerous nuisance. Campfires attract unwanted wildlife, such as

smoky campfire

pesky bears. The fire and smoke obscure your view of the sur-roundings. Evening skies and birds become invisible. When you light a campfire, your world becomes very small, bounded by the light of the fire. Enlarge your world. For a cleaner environment and cleaner, fresher-smelling campers, forego campfires. Instead, use a clean, fast, portable stove for cooking, and provide light as needed with candle lanterns and flashlights.

The high country everywhere is marred with ugly campfire rings. At high elevations in wilderness areas and national parks, where campfires are now illegal, we dismantle old fire rings.

To dismantle fire rings:

- First remove the rocks and move them away from the fire area. Place them some distance apart, in natural-looking positions. Settle them, burnt side down, well into the soil or gravel.
- Pick up litter and pack it out.
- Disperse the ashes over a wide area, well away from water sources.
- Naturalize the area by sprinkling it with soil and gravel.

Stove and Fuel

Each adult member of your party should practice setting up and lighting your portable stove at home, before your camping trip. Know how to adjust, clean, and repair the stove.

Take plenty of fuel. Keep track of how much you use, for future reference. Write down how much fuel you packed, then record how much you brought home at the end of the trip. Note in your travel journal or travel file the amount of fuel you actual-ly used.

Using the home-dried one-pot meal system, you'll need less fuel, since you aren't cooking food, just heating it. We carry a 33-

ounce canister of white gas for a 10-day backpack trip for two people, and always return home with the canister at least a third full.

If you will be melting snow or treating your drinking water by boiling it for three minutes, take plenty of extra fuel—eight ounces of extra gas per day for every one or two campers.

Hot Meals

When you have a full day on the trail ahead of you, start the morning with a quick cold breakfast, break for cold food at lunch, and have your one hot meal late in the afternoon or early in the evening. If a storm appears imminent, you can heat your main meal at noon. In the evening, snack on cold luncheon food while tucked inside your tent. Avoid spilling food on your tent or other equipment. Keep a sponge and water handy for spot cleanup.

Menu Plan

A menu plan lets you take exactly the food you need, with no gaps and no overload. Planning ensures varied, filling, packer-pleasing meals. Over a weeklong trip, try a few hot breakfasts in between cold ones, and have some variety at dinnertime. Don't serve beans or chicken two nights in a row. Avoid perishable fresh foods; instead, carry nonperishable dried meals. Discard

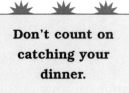

Don't count on catching your dinner.

bread or cheese if it becomes moldy. On long trips, compact crackers or chapatis pack better and stay fresher than yeast breads. Take wax-coated cheeses during long or hot-weather trips. (See Storing Food, Chapter 1, for cheese-preserving methods.) Bring all of the food that you estimate you will need. Don't count on catching your dinner—a frustrating experience if the trout aren't plentiful and

	Wednesday	Thursday	Friday	Saturday	Sunday
Breakfast		Crunchiest Granola with milk and raisins ▸――――――――▸			
		Coffee and tea ▸――――――――――――――――――――▸			
Snack	(pack in late A.M.)	Toffee Bars ▸――――――――――――――――――――▸			
Lunch	Peanut Chapatis; Cheese; Sweet and Sour Jerky ▸――――▸				(pack out late A.M.)
Snack	Dried fruit and nuts ▸――――――――――――――――▸				
	Lemonade mix ▸――――――――――――――――――――▸				
Dinner	Shrimp and Corn Chowder	Hi-Pro Spaghetti	Chicken Caliente	Marcia's Broadway Chili	
	Crispy Crackers			Crispy Crackers	

active. Unless you are an expert, gathering and eating wild plants can be dangerous. At best, gathering and cooking wild plants such as greens and onions is time-consuming, and the food is not filling or nutritious enough to warrant the effort.

Without a menu plan and measured servings of food, you are just guessing how much food you will need. If you pack too little food, you could be left hungry while stranded for days from any food source. Carrying too much food means you will unnecessarily carry extra weight throughout your trip.

The problems of taking not enough or too much food can be avoided if you take a few minutes to write a menu plan prior to your trip. Don't guess at serving sizes; measure the servings so you will have just enough food. Take exactly the meals and snacks you need, plus a couple of lightweight emergency foods.

> **Take a few minutes to write a menu plan prior to your trip.**

Draw a grid menu plan, showing three meals plus two snacks per day in summer, or three meals plus at least three snacks per day in cold weather. On the menu, list the total number of servings of multiple items. As you bag the food, label the bags for the first day as breakfast #1, lunch #1, and dinner #1 by slipping easy-to-read squares of paper into the bags. Continue numbering all of the meals. Then separate the meals into four large plastic bags labeled breakfast, lunch, dinner, and snacks. Attach labels written in waterproof ink to the bags or use different colored bags. Always include a small emergency supply of food that includes at least one sugar snack and one dinner apiece. Label it Emergency. Check off the servings of food as you pack them. Some foods, such as cheese, can be stored in the refrigerator until you leave the house. Write a large note to yourself. Leave the note on top of your backpack so you don't forget any foods that are still in the refrigerator.

The preceding menu plan will feed two people during a four-night backpack trip. All of the recipes are included in this book (see Index).

Total number of servings of multiple items:

- 8 servings granola
- 8 servings coffee and tea
- 8 servings Toffee Bars
- 8 servings Peanut Chapatis
- 8 servings cheese
- 8 servings Sweet and Sour Jerky
- 8 servings dried fruit and nuts
- 8 servings lemonade mix
- 4 servings Crispy Crackers
- 2 servings emergency snacks
- 2 servings emergency dinners

(See Storing Food, Chapter 1, for selecting and preserving cheeses and carrying fragile foods such as crackers and cookies.)

Always carry some emergency food (such as crackers or cookies stored in a tin) in your vehicle. Carry plenty of treated water as well. After your backpack trip, some ready-to-eat food will be welcome and keep you from going hungry if, for example, your vehicle's battery has failed and you must wait for help at the trailhead.

Try some of the following home-dried dinners on your next backpack trip.

Hi-Pro Spaghetti

4 servings

This is fast.

1. Cook, then drain in a colander:

   12 ounces linguine or any pasta

2. Replace pasta in pot, then add and heat gently:

   1 (15-ounce) can whole kernel corn, drained

   1 (15-ounce) can ranch-style beans

   3½ cups tomato sauce

   Sea salt and hot sauce to taste

3. See Home-Dried One-Pot Meals, Chapter 1, for dehydrating instructions.

4. Spread food on plastic-covered dehydrator trays and dehydrate for 6½ hours at 145° F.

5. To rehydrate, cover with water, boil, stir, and serve.

Chicken Caliente

4 servings

This is spicy.

1. Cook, then drain in a colander:

   10 ounces fusilli (corkscrew) pasta

   Set aside.

2. Heat in a large, heavy skillet over medium heat:

   2 tablespoons canola oil

   When the oil is hot, add and stir until very lightly browned:

   1 onion, minced

Add and cook 5 minutes longer, stirring occasionally:
   4 boneless, skinless chicken breast halves, sliced into
   small, thin strips

3. Add and simmer, covered, for 15 minutes:
   2 cups any salsa (Note: For a less spicy dish,
      use 1 cup of salsa and 2 cups of chopped toma-
      toes.)
   1 cup chopped tomatoes, fresh or canned
   ½ cup minced black olives
   ⅓ cup dry red wine
   ½ teaspoon sea salt

4. Blend cooked, drained pasta with chicken mixture.

5. See Home-Dried One-Pot Meals, Chapter 1, for
   dehydrating instructions.

6. Spread pasta-chicken mixture on plastic-covered dehydrator trays and dehydrate for 5 hours at 145° F.

7. To rehydrate, cover with water, boil, stir, and serve.

Mushroom Frittata

4 servings

Vary your menu with a hot breakfast.

1. Heat an ovenproof skillet over medium heat. Add:
   2 teaspoons olive oil
   When the oil is hot, add and cook, stirring, for
   5 minutes:
   2 onions, finely chopped
   Add and cook for 15 minutes, stirring occasionally:
   2 pounds mushrooms, finely chopped
   2 cloves garlic, minced

2. Preheat broiler.

3. Beat together in a large bowl:

   4 whole eggs plus 4 egg whites

   ⅓ cup minced fresh parsley

   ¼ teaspoon sea salt

   ½ teaspoon freshly ground black pepper

   ½ cup finely grated Parmesan cheese

4. Stir the onion-mushroom mixture into the egg mixture.

5. Return the skillet to the stove top. Reduce heat to medium low. Add:

   2 teaspoons olive oil

   When the oil is hot, add the egg mixture. Cook without stirring for 5 minutes.

6. Place the skillet under the preheated broiler for 3 minutes, or until the frittata looks light brown and puffy.

7. See Home-Dried One-Pot Meals, Chapter 1, for dehydrating instructions.

8. Spread the frittata on plastic-covered dehydrator trays and dehydrate for 4 hours at 145° F.

9. To rehydrate, barely cover with water, boil, stir, and serve with Peanut Chapatis (see the following recipe) or Crispy Crackers (see Chapter 7).

Peanut Chapatis

1 dozen chapatis

These stack neatly and keep well.

1. Combine in a medium bowl:

   1¾ cups whole wheat flour

   ¼ cup unbleached white flour

Chapatis are Indian flat breads that are perfect for camping.

¼ teaspoon sea salt

¼ teaspoon paprika

2. Cut in:

   4 teaspoons chilled butter or margarine

   2 teaspoons peanut butter

3. Add slowly, mixing to form a soft dough:

   ⅔ cup cold water

   Knead until smooth.

4. Cover and let stand for 1 hour.

5. Heat griddle to medium.

6. Knead the dough briefly and divide it into 12 pieces.

7. On a floured board, roll out the chapatis as thin as possible into rough circles about 7 inches in diameter.

8. Bake on griddle, turning them frequently, until very light brown.

9. To pack for traveling, let them cool. Cover with foil, then seal in a plastic bag.

   Heat, wrapped in foil, over stove or campfire, if you choose. They taste fine when served unheated.

Journal

A few notes written at the end of each day while backpacking will greatly help with future trip planning. Note how many hours you hiked and the locations where you started and finished each day. Briefly summarize your day. What was special about it? Describe and sketch unfamiliar plants and animals and look them up when you get home. Write a poem.

When you read your journal later, even problems become nostalgic memories. This historical record will be enjoyed by you, and perhaps your heirs, for years to come. No day spent backpacking lacks intensity or beauty.

3

RELAXED CAR
CAMPING

The desert hot spring burbled softly all night, soothing and pleasant. We were camped in an empty Great Basin valley enjoying the sage-scented air. During the long springtime evening a low-flying Cooper's hawk hunted up and down the marshy creek flowing from the spring. The next day we moved on to view a cave filled with ancient pictographs and soaked in another fabulous hot spring.

✳ ✳ ✳

Car camping offers wonderful outdoor experiences for anyone of any age and ability. Your car camping trip can be as energetic or as relaxing as you wish. The choice is yours. Maximize your vacation time by planning your car camping trips just as thoughtfully as your other outdoor adventures.

See more with only a small addition of mileage by planning a car camping loop trip. Shun the boring major highways. Drive on quiet, scenic back roads for extra pleasure and local color. Investigate camping possibilities in your chosen area before you leave home. Attractions that particularly appeal to you may be located in or next to campgrounds. These features can be made the centerpiece of your trip. Instead of aimless long-distance driving, consider your interests and build your next car camping trip around a favorite theme. You don't need to travel far from home to enjoy some or all of the following:

- Day hikes
- Swimming (ocean beaches, lakes, rivers, pools, hot springs)
- Paddling
- Fishing
- Bicycling

- Mountain climbing
- Wildflowers
- Wildlife viewing
- Public gardens
- Historic sites
- Art exhibits and performances

Consider the forms of recreation offered at the campgrounds you choose. Special highlights might tempt you to stay longer. Interesting hiking trails may be located in or near the campground. Fishing, swimming, or boating may be available. Consider the facilities offered when you choose campgrounds. You might prefer primitive camping, with no treated water or flush toilets. Perhaps you are in the mood for the solitude of a walk-in campsite, or you'd like more civilized amenities such as hot showers and ranger-led walks and nature talks.

Camping in National Parks

When you decide to center your trip around a national park, reserve a campsite well in advance. Find up-to-date information about individual United States National Parks on the Park Service home page on the Internet: www.nps.gov. Call MISTIX at (800) 365-2267 to reserve a National Park Service campsite. The big parks, such as

Yellowstone and Yosemite, may be booked months—or even a year—in advance, especially if you need a site during the months of July or August. For Canadian National Parks, you can find information on the Internet at the Great Outdoor Recreation Pages Web site at www.gorp.com in their Canadian Resource Listings. Plan well ahead for your special vacation.

State and Provincial Parks

Most of us have visited some of the famous national parks of North America, but few of us know our other natural treasures such as the state and provincial parks, national monuments, recreation areas, national preserves, and national historical sites that are part of the National Park Service. These lesser-known sites feature all

Big Bend National Park, Texas

types of year-round recreation, including uncrowded camping. Explore these parks via state and provincial guidebooks and on the Internet at: camping.guide@miningco.com. Check the Internet at www.gorp.com in GORP's "Canada by Province" listings. You'll find ideas for trail hiking and for camping in both Provincial Parks and private campgrounds.

Bureau of Land Management and Forest Service Campgrounds

The Bureau of Land Management (BLM) and the United States Forest Service offer thousands of splendid recreation sites, many with free or low-cost camping. These are our favorite car camping choices. They are generally uncrowded and inexpensive, and walking trails or quiet dirt roads and wildlife viewing are often featured. Find complete, up-to-date information about campgrounds in your chosen area by searching the Bureau of Land Management campgrounds at their Web site, www.blm.gov. Research United States Forest Service campgrounds through the United States Department of Agriculture Forest Service Recreation home page at www.fs.fed.us or call the National Recreation Reservation Center at (800) 280-CAMP.

City and County Campgrounds

Often tucked away in a park at the edge of the city limits or hidden in a corner of the city's fairgrounds, local public campgrounds are neglected by most tourists. Find small city and county campgrounds by inquiring at the city hall, or ask any local people. These campgrounds often provide showers and inexpensive camping in an intimate atmosphere. While staying in a town, you can visit the local museum, find information at the library, and make new friends in the café. When I complimented the caretaker of an oak-shaded small-town Texan city camping park, he smiled, "We-all try to keep things nice for you-all."

Other Camping Choices

Discover little-known campgrounds. Check the guidebooks for the state or province of your destination. Many guidebooks are devoted exclusively to public and private campground listings. Buy a guide and greatly expand your camping horizons. You will find campgrounds that are hidden gems.

Sam Houston Jones State Park, Louisiana

While national park campgrounds are heavily booked, often a year in advance, other public campgrounds are far more available. If you hope to stay at a particular camp- ground as a jumping-off place for a spe- cial adventure, reserve a space by contact- ing them in advance.

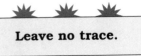

Leave no trace.

In general, your best methods of finding a good campground space are simple:

Gearhart
Mountain
Wilderness,
Oregon

- Camp off-season whenever you can.
- Arrive at campgrounds early, by mid-afternoon.
- Seek out-of-the-way places. Dirt roads and lack of treated water deter many campers. Five to 10 gallons of treated water carried in your vehicle at all times give you more camping choices. You can camp in an "official" site with or without running water, or in an "unofficial" site. If you carry plenty of water, use a portable stove, pack out all of your garbage, and practice cat sanitation for your waste disposal, you are self-contained. When you camp outside of parks or official campgrounds, take extra care to maintain a neat, low profile. Dispose of waste properly. Leave no trace.

Keep Equipment Simple

Car camping is for everyone. You don't need to be an athlete. You don't need to buy expensive equipment. For summer camping in reasonably good weather, the equipment you need is probably already in your possession.

If you will be sleeping on the ground, first cover the ground with a large sheet of plastic, any type of ground cloth, or several large plastic bags, then lay a couple of large, flattened cardboard boxes over the plastic as insulation. If you don't have a mattress or

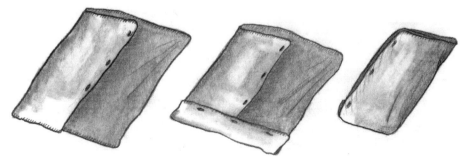

Use some blankets as a lightweight sleeping bag.

**Navajo National
Monument, Arizona**

a sleeping pad, fold several blankets to create a sleeping cushion on top of the cardboard.

You don't need a sleeping bag; you can make one in minutes using blankets and large safety, diaper, or horse blanket pins. Here's how: Spread two or three full-sized blankets and a sheet on your ground cloth or sheet of plastic. Fold the top sheet or blanket over, lengthwise, one-third of the way. Pin the blanket along the sides with three large safety, diaper, or horse blanket pins. Fold up the bottom of the blanket five inches and pin it. Fold the other third of the blanket over the first and pin it. Repeat the process with the second and third blankets, layering them over the first.

You don't need a mess kit or elaborate cooking equipment. Just use unbreakable dishware and old pots and pans from your home kitchen. Take sturdy, all-metal pots, such as steel, cast-iron, or heavy aluminum that won't melt in a hot fire.

If you lack a tent, take an inexpensive grommeted tarp and some nylon cord. Improvise a lean-to shelter.

The clothing you need is already in your closet. Take old clothes that you don't mind tearing or staining. Wear your old clothes while in camp, and reserve at least one "good" set of clothing. Try your first car camping trip during dry, bug-free weather. Use bedding and cooking equipment from your home. As you gain camping experience, define your needs and borrow, rent, or buy basic camping equipment, one piece at a time.

After some camping experience, when you are ready to buy a sleeping bag, tent, and portable stove, you will have a good idea of what you need. Buy lightweight, multipurpose, and excellent-quality gear. If your equipment is both lightweight and durable, you can take it on all your boating, skiing, car camping, or backpacking adventures. It will last.

Car Camp Kitchen

The light was fading when we pulled into the public campground, so we didn't waste time preparing dinner. We pulled out our portable stove, a small pot, and a packet of home-dried Long Trail Lentils. A few minutes later we were enjoying a hot meal. Another group of campers had arrived at the same time. We noticed while we were eating dinner that they were still struggling to get their smoky campfire going. They finally sat down to dinner more than an hour later.

✳   ✳   ✳

Try using a portable stove—and home-dried meals, or quick-cooking fresh foods—instead of a campfire for convenience, cleaner air, and cleaner campers. A supply of home-dried meals makes camp dinners easy and tasty. Here are some recipes to cook at home for quick meals when you're on vacation.

Long Trail Lentils

4 servings

This is easy to cook and dehydrate.

1. Preheat oven to 325° F.
2. Mix together in a 9 by 13-inch glass casserole dish:

   5 cups vegetable, chicken, seafood, or beef stock

   1 cup rinsed, uncooked lentils

   ¾ cup rinsed, uncooked brown rice

   1 onion, finely chopped

   10 fresh mushrooms, finely chopped

   4 cloves garlic, minced

   1 jalapeño pepper, fresh or canned, seeded and minced, or hot sauce to taste

   2 teaspoons minced fresh thyme, or 1 teaspoon dried

   ½ teaspoon sea salt
3. Cover and bake for 1 hour.
4. Uncover the casserole and stir it. Sprinkle over the top:

   ½ cup finely grated Gruyère cheese

   Return the casserole to the oven and bake, uncovered, 10 minutes longer.
5. See Home-Dried One-Pot Meals, Chapter 1, for dehydrating instructions.
6. Spread the casserole on plastic-covered dehydrator trays and dehydrate for 3 hours at 145° F.
7. To rehydrate, cover with water, boil, stir, and serve.

Carrot-Apple Soup

4 servings

1. Heat a cast-iron Dutch oven over medium heat. Add:

   2 tablespoons canola oil

   When the oil is hot, add and cook, stirring, until soft:

   2 onions, finely chopped

   3 cloves garlic, minced

2. Add and cook for 20 minutes longer:

   6 carrots, chopped

   3 tart, unpeeled apples, chopped

   2 teaspoons ground ginger

   ½ teaspoon ground white pepper

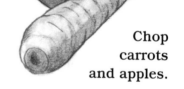

3. Add and bring to a boil:

   5½ cups any variety stock or water

   1 whole bay leaf

   Simmer for 40 minutes. Turn off heat; let cool slightly.

Chop carrots and apples.

4. Whirl soup in blender until smooth. Replace soup in pot. Add and stir:

   1 cup nonfat milk

   ¼ teaspoon sea salt

5. See Home-Dried One-Pot Meals, Chapter 1, for dehydrating instructions.

6. Spread soup on plastic-covered dehydrator trays and dehydrate for 6 hours at 145° F.

7. To rehydrate, cover with water, boil, stir, and serve with Peanut Chapatis (see Chapter 2) or Crispy Crackers (see Chapter 7).

Roasted Vegetable Spread

4 servings

**No heating is required in the field.
To rehydrate, simply add water. Use as a dip
or a sandwich spread.**

1. Preheat oven to 450° F.
2. Mix together in a cast-iron Dutch oven, or other baking pan with a lid, stirring thoroughly to coat:

    2 tablespoons olive oil

    4 large onions, finely chopped

    1 large eggplant, finely chopped

    8 cloves garlic, minced
3. Bake vegetables, covered, in oven for 30 minutes. Stir, then bake, uncovered, for 30 minutes longer, or until browned.
4. Whirl in a blender or food processor along with the roasted vegetables:

    1½ cups plain nonfat yogurt

    1 teaspoon freshly ground pepper

    ½ teaspoon sea salt
5. See Home-Dried One-Pot Meals, Chapter 1, for dehydrating instructions.
6. Spread vegetable mixture on plastic-covered dehydrator trays and dehydrate for 4 hours at 145° F.
7. To rehydrate, add a little water and stir until dip consistency is obtained. Let stand for 1 minute. Serve as a dip with Crispy Crackers (see Chapter 7) or spread on Peanut Chapatis (see Chapter 2).

Canned and Dried Foods

Keep a supply of canned and dried foods ready to heat. A hot dish, such as a soup or a stew, makes a quick, complete dinner when combined with bread and a salad. With a few cans of corn and garbanzo beans, the following soup is ready to eat in minutes.

Zippy Corn Soup

4 servings

1. Mix together in a large pot:

    2 (15-ounce) cans creamed corn

    2 (15-ounce) cans garbanzo beans

    2 cups water

    ½ cup nonfat dry milk

    Sea salt and freshly ground black pepper or hot sauce,
        to taste

2. Heat until almost boiling. Serve with bread and salad.

Fat-Free Salad Dressing

Try some fast, fat-free salad dressing: sprinkle balsamic, wine, or cider vinegar and seasoned salt or salt-free seasoning over prepared greens. You won't even miss the oil.

Chutney Cheese Toast

4 servings

1. Toast on one side:

   8 slices bread

2. Turn the slices and cover the toasted sides with:

   4 tablespoons chutney

   1 cup grated sharp cheese

   1 tomato, thinly sliced

   Freshly ground black pepper

3. Toast until the cheese melts.

chutney

Quick-to-Prepare Foods That Store Well

For car camping, choose simple foods that keep well:

- Flat breads: crackers, melba toast, chapatis, pita bread, and tortillas

- Long-keeping, dense breads: pumpernickel, raisin bread, bannock bread, and canned Boston brown bread

- Quick grains: pasta, polenta, couscous, kasha, quick rice, bulgur, and grits

- Canned or dried foods: beans, soups, stews, fruits, vegetables, meats, fish, and sauces

- Fresh vegetables and fruits that store well for days, even without refrigeration: root vegetables (such as carrots, jicama, or potatoes), cabbage, apples. Keep fruits and vegetables well wrapped in a cool, dark place. Use them as stir-fried vegetables or as salads.

- Dry salami, beef, fish, or other jerkies, hard cheese, peanut butter, honey, and jelly
- Instant dry milk, cereals, cocoa, coffee, tea, drink mixes. Improve the flavor of dry milk by mixing it with water, then storing it overnight in an ice chest. Serve the milk with breakfast.

> **Frozen jugs of water will be ready for last-minute camping trips and they help your freezer operate more efficiently.**

Ice Chest

Your own frozen jugs of water last far longer and are less messy than purchased blocks of ice—and you can drink the ice water. At home, nearly fill one or two screw-top one-gallon plastic jugs with water. Leave three inches of room for the water to expand when it freezes. Place the jugs in your freezer. These jugs of ice will be ready for last-minute camping trips, and they help your freezer operate more efficiently. Always keep some on hand.

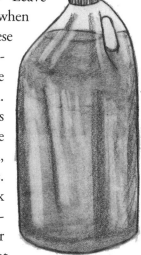

For camping trips, place the frozen jugs in the ice chest along with your perishable foods. Upon arrival at your campground, drain the melted ice water into drinking cups. Replace the drained ice in the chest. Drink the ice water as is or stir in your choice of powdered drink mix. If you drain the ice water daily in cool weather and twice a day in hot weather, a gallon jug of ice will last for three

frozen water jug

or four days. Keep your ice chest in a cool, shady spot. Insulate it with blankets and pillows during the day.

Prepare home-cooked meals in advance and freeze them for use during the first day of your camping trip. At home, place the cooked food in waxed cartons such as clean recycled milk or juice cartons. Double-bag the food in plastic bags and label it: name of the dish, how many servings, date it was made. Store the food in your home freezer. For camping, take along one of the frozen meals. Store the carton upright in the corner of your ice chest along with a frozen jug of water. To avoid foodborne illness, use the frozen meal as soon as it thaws, the first evening of your camping trip.

When you run out of ice, use any food that might spoil immediately, or discard it. Fresh foods that can spoil and make you ill include the protein foods such as meat, eggs, milk, soft

**King Lear Peak,
Nevada**

cheese, and cooked beans. Keep the lid off your ice chest until you are able to buy more ice. If you keep the ice chest aired, it won't become musty. Bag your remaining less perishable provisions in plastic or paper bags. Cover them with wet cloths and store them in your ice chest without the lid. Evaporation from the wet cloths will keep your food surprisingly cool.

Sleep Comfortably

Our favorite time of year for car camping is autumn. The crowds and mosquitoes are gone. The colorful foliage and migrating birds are spectacular. Check your guidebook or the Internet to be sure your chosen campgrounds have not closed for the season. Even in early November in northern areas, you can sleep cozily outdoors. If you don't have sleeping bags, take flannel sheets and plenty of warm blankets. Fold and pin the blankets to create a sleeping bag. (See Keep Equipment Simple, this chapter.)

> Car camping in autumn helps you avoid the crowds and the mosquitoes, plus the colorful foliage and migrating birds are spectacular.

If it is very cold, heat some water and fill a hot water bottle and place it in the foot of your bed during the evening. Most cold comes up from the ground rather than from the air. Add some extra insulation underneath your mattress or sleeping pad. Tarps, several layers of newspaper, flattened cardboard boxes, or blankets insulate you from the ground.

hot water bottle

CAR CAMPING LIST

Shelter

- ☐ Backpack, if needed for walk-in campsites or backpack trips. Store backpack gear inside the backpack and replace gear when you're through using it.
- ☐ Daypack
- ☐ Tent
  - ☐ Fly
  - ☐ Poles
  - ☐ Stakes + 2 extra
- ☐ Sleeping bag and stuff sacks (or sheets and blankets)
- ☐ Sleeping pad (or foam mattress or extra folded blankets)
- ☐ Ground cloth (or large plastic bags)
- ☐ Pillow
- ☐ 50-foot nylon cord
- ☐ Small stack of old newspapers
- ☐ Flattened cardboard boxes
- ☐ Paper and plastic bags, assorted sizes

Clothing

- ☐ Boots
  - ☐ Insoles
- ☐ Athletic shoes
- ☐ Sandals
- ☐ Sunglasses
- ☐ Brimmed hat
- ☐ Knit cap
- ☐ Mosquito head net
- ☐ Waterproof jacket and pants
- ☐ Lightweight synthetic gloves
- ☐ Mittens or heavyweight gloves
- ☐ Bandana
- ☐ Sweater
- ☐ Sweat suit
- ☐ Medium-weight synthetic long underwear
- ☐ 2 pairs trousers
- ☐ Nylon belt
- ☐ Belt pack
- ☐ 3 pairs heavy socks
- ☐ 3 pairs liner socks
- ☐ Extra pairs medium-weight socks
- ☐ 2 long-sleeved lightweight shirts
- ☐ 2 short-sleeved lightweight shirts
- ☐ 4 cotton or synthetic T-shirts
- ☐ 1 heavy wool or synthetic shirt

CAR CAMPING LIST (CONTINUED)

- [ ] 2 turtleneck shirts
- [ ] 4 pairs underpants
- [ ] Nylon shorts
- [ ] Swimsuit

Safety and Route Finding

- [ ] Whistle
- [ ] Flashlight
  - [ ] Extra batteries
- [ ] Matches, including water- and windproof matches in a match safe
- [ ] Paper, pen, and pencil
- [ ] Wristwatch
- [ ] Pocketknife
- [ ] Compass
- [ ] Maps, road atlas
- [ ] Binoculars
- [ ] Phone numbers and addresses
- [ ] Credit card, cash, including coins for campground showers and telephone
- [ ] Candle to start emergency campfire

- [ ] Folding shovel or sturdy trowel

Toiletries

- [ ] Toilet paper
- [ ] Comb and brush
- [ ] Sunscreen
- [ ] Tube of petroleum jelly
- [ ] Aloe vera cream
- [ ] Hand cream
- [ ] Lip balm with sunscreen
- [ ] Insect repellent
- [ ] Benzocaine for insect bites
- [ ] Premoistened wipes
- [ ] Cotton or synthetic towel
- [ ] Soap
- [ ] Shampoo
- [ ] Toothbrush
- [ ] Toothpaste
- [ ] Dental floss
- [ ] Toothpicks
- [ ] Multivitamins
- [ ] Personal medications

First Aid

- [ ] Bandages
- [ ] Gauze pads

CAR CAMPING LIST (CONTINUED)

- ☐ Elastic bandage
- ☐ Tweezers
- ☐ Aspirin
- ☐ Antihistamine
- ☐ Bismuth tablets
- ☐ Salt
- ☐ Baking soda

Repair Kit

- ☐ 2 needles
- ☐ Thread
- ☐ Rip-stop tape
- ☐ Duct tape
- ☐ Safety pins
- ☐ Rubber bands
- ☐ Extra flashlight bulb
- ☐ Metal rings for packs
- ☐ Fishing line and hooks
- ☐ Tent pole repair sleeve
- ☐ Light- and heavyweight zipper repair kits
- ☐ Compact tool kit that includes pliers and screwdrivers

Foot Kit

- ☐ 2nd Skin
- ☐ Moleskin
- ☐ Rubbing alcohol
- ☐ Scissors
- ☐ Micropore tape
- ☐ Lamb's wool
- ☐ Bandages
- ☐ Needle
- ☐ Matches
- ☐ Nail clippers

Food and Water

- ☐ Water filter or purification tablets. Borrow or buy a good microporous filter, boil all your drinking water for three minutes, or use iodine tablets. Never drink untreated water.
- ☐ Ice chest
- ☐ Canteens and belt holder
- ☐ Large jugs filled with treated water (a total of 5 to 10 gallons of water)
- ☐ Collapsible water jug
- ☐ Collapsible bucket

CAR CAMPING LIST (CONTINUED)

- ☐ Solar shower
- ☐ Portable stove
- ☐ Full container of fuel
- ☐ Extra fuel
- ☐ Aluminum pot and lid
- ☐ Skillet
- ☐ Unbreakable plates, cups, and bowls, including Sierra cups
- ☐ Sheathed knife
- ☐ Silverware
- ☐ Bottle and can openers
- ☐ Corkscrew
- ☐ Wooden spoon
- ☐ Spatula
- ☐ Small cutting board
- ☐ Grater
- ☐ Salt
- ☐ Chili powder

- ☐ Liquid soap
- ☐ Nylon net
- ☐ Sponge
- ☐ 2 dish towels
- ☐ Thermos

Personal

- ☐ Keys, house and vehicle
- ☐ Camera
  - ☐ Extra film
- ☐ Books, magazines, nature guides
- ☐ Frisbee, deck of cards, or other simple games
- ☐ Gas or candle lantern
- ☐ Citronella candle
- ☐ Hot water bottle
- ☐ Portable chairs

Let Your Vehicle Wash Your Clothes

Use a tightly covered plastic bucket, such as a detergent container. In the morning, mix some soap and water in the bucket, add clothes, cover, and secure the bucket to keep it from tipping inside

Fort Rock, Oregon

your vehicle. After hours of driving, your clothes will be agitated clean. Upon arrival at your campground in the afternoon, rinse the clothes, then dry them overnight.

Candles

In cold, soaking wet conditions, candles are better than matches for starting emergency campfires. They are handy on any camping trip. Store them in a cool, well-wrapped place in your vehicle or pack. Burning candles are unsafe inside tents or vehicles but are perfect for picnic tables, tailgates, or set on mineral soil on the ground outside your tent.

To make a candle lantern, cut the top off a tin can. Place a votive candle in a glass holder inside the can. Weight the bottom of the can with a couple of rocks. Be careful; the can will get hot after the candle's been burning for a while. Use it only on nonflammable surfaces.

Use a tin can as a candle lantern.

Newspapers

Carry a bag full of newspapers and paper bags under the seats in your vehicle. Use them as:

- Emergency fire starter
- Insulation under sleeping bags or mattress
- Seating pads
- Tablecloth
- Folded as paper sandwich plates

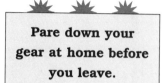

Pare down your gear at home before you leave.

Closed-Cell Foam Pads

These pads are lightweight, compact, and shed water. They are most often used as sleeping pads, but they can also serve as extra seating. Use them as lounges. You can sit or lie on the ground, bend them up against a rock, or pad and warm a cold, hard, or damp log, tailgate, or picnic bench.

Valuables

closed-cell foam pad

When you must leave sleeping bags and other valuable items in your vehicle, keep them out of sight. I like to throw a couple of ancient, rumpled tarps over everything in the vehicle, making it an unappealing target for potential thieves. The tarps also hide the ice chest from the view of curious bears.

Getting Comfortable

During long car camping trips, we find that we truly prefer sleeping outdoors to renting a room at night. We enjoy eating simple meals outdoors more than eating in restaurants. We prefer this because the rhythm of the outdoors is more beautiful and relaxing. There's so much more to see and do when you are living outdoors.

During many years of camping we have learned to camp simply and neatly, so work is minimized and fun time maximized. When you follow our plan, you will find that your equipment is clean, tidy, and kept in its place. You will spend little time cleaning, straightening, and looking for misplaced gear. No bear or raccoon will be attracted to dirty dishes lying around your camp; you've cleaned the dishes after your meal and slipped them back into your equipment box.

Don't take excess gear.

Here are the easy rules for neat and simple camping.

- Don't take anything that you don't use frequently. Carry only pieces of equipment that you use at least every other day. If it isn't used, leave it at home next time.

- While in camp, return your gear to the same place every time. Don't set it down on a rock or a log. Put it back in the equipment box.

- Keep a low profile with a neat, litter-free campsite and vehicle. You will blend into the wilderness, your camp will look more natural to you and to anyone else who sees it, and you will be able to find your gear more easily.

At the provincial park in Nova Scotia, our neighboring campers seemed to be carrying everything they owned. Their van bulged with stuff, and much more was precariously strapped to the vehicle's roof. An unused rocking horse rode on top of the heap. We thought they were moving house, but no, they were en vacances. They spent their campground stay rummaging through their piles of clutter.

✳   ✳   ✳

You will have fewer items to pack into the vehicle, to sort through while you're camping, and to unpack and store at home. Analyze your gear. If you really love your folding chairs, bring them along. Do you usually pack a large but little-used charcoal barbecue just because your dad always took one camping? Leave it at home.

One of the great pleasures of living outdoors is enjoying yourself without the accoutrements of modern life. Keep it light, stay comfortable, and surround yourself with only the gear you truly need and love.

4

CAMPING WITH CHILDREN

I glanced at my watch and smiled. Cathie had been follow-ing the caterpillars' progress for two hours. This warm spring day had brought out dozens of woolly bear caterpillars. Cathie crouched, fascinated, as the fuzzy insects munched plantain leaves in the marshy area below our camp. Cathie, like other young children entranced with the natural world, doesn't need to be entertained with the peak climbs or sweeping views favored by adults in the camping party. A chipmunk sighting is just as thrilling to her as a bull moose sighting.

A child's first camping trip will forever influence the way she views the outdoors. Make that first experience short, easy, and positive. When planning your adventure, think child-centered, not adult. You may enjoy 10 challenging miles of rocky cross-country scram-bling, but your toddler will prefer a brief half-mile hike to a lake on soft, groomed trail. If you want to communicate love of the out-doors to your children, slow down. Let the children in the party set the pace, not the adults. Enjoy your child's sense of wonder. Plan for games, songs, and cups of cocoa. Keep it short and simple.

Prepared Parents

Children are natural campers. They find more to do and see outdoors than less imaginative adults, but they do need to be kept safe and comfortable. Cold, tired, sunburned, or mosquito-bitten children will not enjoy their wilderness experience. Children expect fun on a vacation, and nothing but fun. Adults can shrug off a few discomforts, but children don't understand why you go camping if camping isn't a pleasure.

> The adults in a camping party need some camping experience before heading into the wilderness with children.

With young children in your party, keep your trips short, comfortable, and on gentle terrain. Know when to pack up and leave. When the weather turns bad or a child feels ill, you can hike out quickly if you haven't traveled too far. Since the adults in the party will be carrying extra weight, a short trip will be more comfortable for them, too. You don't need to go far to enjoy wonderful family camping trips.

Before heading into the wilderness with children, the adults in the party need some camping experience. If you've never tried car camping or backpacking, go on some trips by yourselves first. Make sure your equipment is satisfactory. Think about sharing this experience with your children. What extra gear would make the trip more pleasant for them? What excess baggage could you leave behind?

For their first experience sleeping outdoors, take your children car camping. When you're ready to spend a night or two sleeping away from your vehicle, invite some other adults with backpacking experience to join you, and invite them to bring their children.

Children need to prepare, too. Here are some tips to get them ready for their first camping trip.

- First let them try "camping out" in the backyard, or even on your living-room floor. They can set up a tent or tarp or a simulated shelter and roll out their sleeping bags or blanket bedrolls at home. (See Keep Equipment Simple, Chapter 3, for bedrolls improvisation and other equipment suggestions.)

- Prepare a camp meal for your children outdoors.

- Try using your portable stove either at a local park or in your backyard.

- Take your children on several all-day outings that include hikes and picnics. These will serve as shakedown cruises for future overnight trips.

- Find small daypacks or fanny packs that are comfortable for your children. Let them carry jackets and snacks in their packs.

- Children need appropriate footwear. You don't need to buy new walking shoes or boots for them. You can borrow or buy used ones at thrift stores or garage sales, but make sure they fit well and provide support.

Where and When to Camp

Your camping destination should provide interest for the child. Go to a place that encourages play. For example, choose a trip near water: a pond, lake, creek, or river, preferably with shallow, slow-moving water for splashing. Children need the open space of beaches or woodland meadows with rocks and trees to climb. Children need plenty of room to safely run around and make noise without disturbing other campers. While driving, paddling, or hiking to your destination, take the frequent breaks that all active children need. Don't confine them to a car or a boat for too long. Stop early each day. If you are car camping and you stop by mid-afternoon, your children will have time for energetic play. Everyone will sleep better at night after fun and exercise around camp.

> **Warm days in late August or early September are the best times for camping with children in most climates.**

Take children camping when the weather is good and the bug problem is minimal. Children feel the cold more than adults, and their delicate skin is more sensitive to insect bites. Warm days in late August or early September are the best times for camping with children in most climates. A cold, rainy, or very buggy weekend crammed inside the tent is no way to spend a family vacation.

Planning with the Whole Family

Involve your child. Everyone likes to feel autonomous. Children will be far more willing to camp if they help initiate and plan the trip instead of being unwillingly dragged along on the adults' expedition.

- Let them help decide where you'll camp. How many nights will you stay? What foods will you take? Children love to dehydrate food. (See Home-Dried One-Pot Meals, Chapter 1, for dehydrating instructions.)
- Let children make cookies, measure individual servings of granola with dry milk and raisins into bags, and create their own trail mix.

- They can help pack. Let them think about what they will need to take. On a backpack trip, give them a daypack and some gear of their own to carry, but not so much weight that they will get overtired.

child-sized daypack

- On the trail, let them lead. They will be happier if they are contributing to the group effort.

- When you set up camp, assign chores to your children. Allow plenty of extra time while they learn basic camping routines.

From the time they're old enough for a short backpack trip, consider bringing a playmate or two for your children. Two children sharing their own tent will have a ball. Plan a family trip on a river or lake. A gentle paddling trip might be more comfortable for toddlers who are unable to walk far. (See Paddling with Children, Chapter 5.)

Protect Children

You're responsible for your children's safety. Don't jeopardize their well-being by foregoing proper equipment in order to backpack carrying less weight. A tent is an essential piece of equipment when taking babies and very young children into the wilderness. Little ones must be protected from sunburn, dehydration, insect bites,

> Sunscreen needs to be absorbed by the skin before it's effective. For adults, give the sunscreen 30 minutes to be absorbed; for children, give it an hour.

and the possibility of hypothermia caused by wind, rain, and cold weather. Even during good weather, children sometimes need to get in out of the wind and rest for a while. Small comforts such as a favorite toy, plenty of flashlight batteries to calm children in the darkness, and tasty, frequent snacks are necessities.

> **Dot clothing with liquid insect repellent.**

Protect children from the sun. Give them sunglasses secured with retainers. Cover heads and necks with adequate hats, and use sunscreen liberally. Sunscreen needs to be absorbed by the skin before it can be effective, so try to apply sunscreen to your children 60 minutes before they will be exposed to the sun. (Adults should apply it 30 minutes before.)

Dot clothing with liquid insect repellent. Apply the repellent to hat brims, shirt collars, and cuffs. Avoid applying it directly to a child's skin. Insect repellent in spray form is likely to get into children's eyes or be inhaled and should not be used.

Offer children plenty of liquids, including a lot of water. Children may not be aware that they are becoming dehydrated. (See Avoid Dehydration and Heatstroke, Chapter 1.)

Camp Rules

Set up imaginary parameters around your campsite. No one in the party should stray from these boundaries without telling the others exactly where they are going and when they will return. Walk these parameters with your children. Point out hazards in the area: slippery mud, leaves or gravel, dead tree limbs that could break if climbed upon, watercourses, poison ivy or oak, or thorny plants.

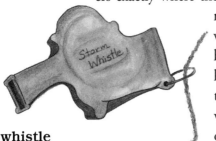

whistle

Each member of the party needs to carry a loud whistle at all times, preferably attached on a clip or cord. It is not a toy and must be used only when calling for help. If someone is separated from the party, one whistle blast means "here I am." Three blasts are the universal emergency signal to request help.

Clothing

Be able to spot your children at a distance. Choose brightly colored camp clothing for them. Take many layers of lightweight clothing for each child. Take at least one full set of extra clothes for each child; protect a set of emergency clothes in a plastic bag. If your child gets thoroughly soaked, get him or her into dry clothes immediately. Be sure children's hats are adequate. Each child needs a wide-brimmed sun hat that protects the face and neck and a warm wool or synthetic hat that ties down over the ears. Monitor babies and toddlers frequently for overheating or chills; add or remove layers of clothing as frequently as required. Infants riding in a child carrier will feel colder than racing, tumbling toddlers.

child's fleece jacket

Weight-Wise Packing

When your party includes an infant or a toddler who must be carried, the weight carried by others in the party will often necessitate a shorter trip. It's unrealistic to pack food for 10 days, and a baby, and baby gear on the backs of a couple of adults. A toddler who is willing to walk but who can carry only a tiny pack must have nearly all of his or her food and clothing, and a sleeping bag and some form of shelter, carried by the rest of the party. This means that one or more of the adults will be carrying almost twice as much weight as usual.

Be ruthless and realistic (see Paring Down, Chapter 2). Weigh yourself and your equipment, adding the weight of your infant or easily-tired toddler who must be carried.

Here are lightweight alternatives for longer, more comfortable backpack trips that include young children in your party:

- Cache food—and diapers—in advance, hidden, along your route. Protect the cached gear in weather- and animal-proof containers.

- Arrange a pickup point where a friend or relative can meet and resupply your party partway through your trip. That person can bring you food and clean clothes and diapers and pack out everything you no longer need.

- Hire a pack llama outfitter, or rent your own llamas, to carry your food, equipment, and toddlers in and out of the backcountry.

- Form a camping party of many adults and few children. Between them, the adults can easily carry the extra gear.

Diapers

Bury baby feces the same way you bury your own (see Human Waste Disposal, Chapter 1). Bring plenty of diapers, preferably a combination of both cloth and disposable diapers. Reserve the disposable diapers for damp or

collapsible bucket

rainy weather. In good weather, use cloth diapers; it's better than carrying a bag full of used disposable ones. Wash the cloth diapers in a collapsible bucket or other separate container; do not use your cooking pot. Air-dry the diapers if you are staying in a base camp. If you're hiking in good weather, use safety pins to fasten the washed cloth diapers to the outside of your pack and let them flap dry as you walk.

Do not bury or burn disposable diapers. Never throw them into a toilet. After burying the feces, double-bag disposable diapers in opaque plastic bags, strap the bags to the outside of your pack, and pack them out.

Study the Outdoors

Make camping a family learning experience. Frightening images of animals such as bears or snakes can be changed to respectful understanding if you buy or borrow library books on pertinent nature topics such as weather, wildlife, and astronomy. A simple tree identification guide will provide hours of pleasure for the whole family during time spent at campsites.

lodgepole pinecone and needles

Weather

Predicting approaching weather is a lifelong challenge. The whole family can practice their skills daily while camping. Keep alert for weather changes. Your observations can help you plan the day's or week's activities, and preparedness could save your life while in the wilderness.

Before your wilderness trip, study the latest weather reports for an overall picture of the weather fronts that are approaching. This knowledge, plus your assessment of the weather prospects in your backcountry surroundings, can keep you aware of upcoming shifts in the weather. Remember that pockets of changeable mountain weather can be different than the overall picture for the region. The mountains create their own weather.

Learn to recognize cloud formations, read the color of the sun and the moon, and understand the meaning of changes in wind direction. A good outdoorsperson can predict approaching weather with a fair degree of accuracy, especially if two or more of the weather-indicating signs listed below are observed. Perhaps you saw a ring around the moon in the evening, followed by a very red sunrise the next morning. Now you notice that the wind is blowing from the south. You'll prepare for a day of rain.

Clouds

The clouds are beautiful, racing across the sky. Are they building up to rain? The shape, elevation, movement, and color of the clouds can tell you. A clear sky, or one with a few high, rising clouds and a light breeze, especially a breeze from the north, indicates good weather. Clouds that thicken, darken, and lower with wind coming out of the west, then coming from the south, can indicate approaching rain.

Puffy *cumulus* clouds indicate fair weather when they are white and few in number. The word *cumulus* means mound. Cumulus clouds are puffy, rounded clouds that form changing pictures in the sky. Watch them carefully for changes. If they turn dark and become more numerous, they may bring showers. When cumulus clouds form a tall black tower, they are called *cumulonimbus* clouds. These dark towers indicate approaching thunderstorms.

Lovely, wispy *cirrus* clouds are nicknamed "mares' tails." When these clouds are pale and float high in the sky, they indicate

"mares' tails"

"mackerel sky"

fair weather. If they darken and move lower in the sky, they can bring rain.

Stratus clouds are high and thin. They can predict a hazy day if they remain high and pale. Observe them carefully for changes. If they thicken and move lower in the sky, rain may be on the way.

Cirrocumulus clouds, which look like fish scales, predict rain, or a rain front passing nearby. "Mackerel sky, rain is nigh."

Sun

A clear, red sunset predicts fair weather. A red sunrise, especially if it's a hazy red, foretells rain. "Red sky at night, sailors' delight; red sky at morning, sailors take warning; red sky at noon, it will rain soon," often within just a few hours.

Moon

Does the moon look bright white? If so, a clear day will follow. A hazy yellow or orange moon indicates humidity and the possibility of rain. "Ring around the moon, it will rain soon." A visible halo of moisture circling the moon is a sign of coming rain.

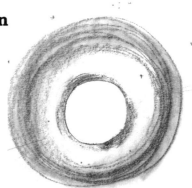

ring around the moon

Wind

"When the wind is in the south, it blows the bait in fishes' mouths." A breeze coming from the south often predicts rain and good fishing weather. If the wind is coming from the southeast in the evening, it could rain by morning. When an updraft causes hardwood (deciduous) trees such as oaks or maples to show the undersides of their leaves, rain is on the way.

Sounds and Odors

Can you hear sounds from far off, such as the twittering of birds far away on the other side of the lake? Is there very little air movement? Are odors from vegetation more pronounced? If so, the cloud cover is thickening, holding down sounds and odors and blocking air movement. These are all signs of approaching rain.

Activities to Continue the Fun

Here are some fun activities that children can do on their own or with an adult or two.

"Fishing" and "Panning for Gold"

Give children fishing rods, or let very young ones pretend to fish. A stick with string attached, a gold pan fashioned from a pie tin, or a small bucket and a shovel will provide hours of pleasure for a child dawdling streamside or oceanside with the adults. Supervise children closely while they are around water; an adult-to-child ratio of one-to-one is best. If your party is equipped with personal flotation devices, let your children wear them when playing near the water as well as when in or on the water. (See Paddling with Children, Chapter 5.)

Camping Children's Reading List

The following books can be enjoyed by children while resting at your campsite or just before bed with a flashlight.

Carlson, Laurie, and Judith Dammel. *Kids Camp! Activities for the Backyard or Wilderness*. Chicago: Chicago Review Press, Inc., 1995.

Cole, Joanna, and Stephanie Calmenson. *Rain or Shine Activity Book*. New York: William Morrow & Co., 1997.

Drake, Jane, and Ann Love. *The Kids Campfire Book*. Toronto: Kids Can Press, 1998.

___. *The Kids Summer Games Book*. Toronto: Kids Can Press, 1998.

George, Jean Craighead. *My Side of the Mountain*. New York: Puffin Books, 1975.

Hawthorne, Nathaniel. *A Wonder Book for Girls and Boys*. New York: Tor Books, 1998.

Kipling, Rudyard; Peter Levi, Ed. *Just So Stories*. New York: Viking Penguin, 1991.

London, Jack. *The Call of the Wild*. New York: Pocket Books, 1982.

MacDonald, Margaret Read. *Twenty Tellable Tales*. New York: H. W. Wilson, 1991.

Paulsen, Gary. *Father Water, Mother Woods*. New York: Dell Publishing Co., 1996.

___. *My Life in Dog Years*. New York: Delacorte Press, 1998.

Poe, Edgar Allan; Graham Clarke, Ed. *Tales of Mystery and Imagination*. Boston: Charles E. Tuttle Co., Inc., 1993.

Russell, William F. *Classics to Read Aloud to Your Children*. New York: Crown Publications, 1992.

___. *More Classics to Read Aloud to Your Children*. New York: Crown Publications, 1994.

San Souci, Robert D. *Short and Shivery*. New York: Doubleday & Co., Inc., 1989.

Camping Children's Reading List (continued)

Schwartz, Alvin. *Scary Stories to Tell in the Dark.* New York: HarperCollins, 1981.

Silverstein, Shel. *Where the Sidewalk Ends: The Poems and Drawings of Shel Silverstein.* New York: HarperCollins, 1974.

Sobey, Ed. *Car Smarts: Activities for Kids on the Open Road.* New York: McGraw-Hill, 1997.

Tashjian, Virginia. *Juba This and Juba That: Stories to Tell, Songs to Sing, Rhymes to Chant, Riddles to Guess and More!* Boston: Little, Brown & Co., 1995.

Games

Bring games everyone can play together, such as a miniature Frisbee made especially for backpacking. A quick game of Frisbee, followed by a few minutes of stretching, helps campers to loosen stiff muscles after a day of hiking. For stormy days inside your tent or camping vehicle, bring simple games, such as a deck of cards. Everyone can play charades. Practice your storytelling skills with round-robin storytelling: one person begins to tell a story, then the next person continues the tale. Always bring books for reading both alone and aloud.

Keep a Journal

Keeping a journal while camping lets children and adults alike take closer note of their surroundings and creatively record their impressions. Take notebook journals for everyone. Draw pictures of the scenery, leaves, or animal tracks. Make notes. Keep a log of animals and plants you have observed. Describe what you did each day. Write a story. Be sure to write the dates in your journal and note where you camped. After many years and many camping trips you will enjoy knowing what year, and where, you wrote each journal.

Binoculars and Magnifying Glass

Find a quiet spot. Get comfortable behind some cover. Observe birds and other wildlife. Examine soil, bugs, and tiny plants up close.

Pressed Leaves

As you hike on the trail or wander around camp, look for interesting leaves lying on the ground. Don't pick living leaves or flowers. Wipe the dirt and moisture off the leaves, then press them between the pages of a magazine. When you get home, put the leaves between weighted sheets of newspaper. Turn and move the leaves daily for about a week or until they are completely dry. Glue the leaves into your journal or onto blank paper. Use as note paper, or fold the paper to make a greeting card.

Press leaves in a magazine.

Baby Food

A small, hand food grinder lets you feed your baby on a backpack trip as easily as you do at home. After you have heated your dehydrated dinner, simply grind a small portion of it for your baby (see Home-Dried One-Pot Meals, Chapter 1). When you camp using your own dehydrated meals, you can control the seasoning so the flavors are appropriate for little ones and acceptable to adults, too; avoid very spicy or strong-flavored foods. Or, you can easily dehydrate pureed foods especially for your baby, such as the following fruit dish.

Baby Peach Treat

8 (½-cup) servings

This is a pureed fruit and cereal dish for babies, children, and adults.

1. Preheat oven to 375° F.
2. Oil a 9 by 13-inch glass casserole dish.
3. Place in the bottom of the dish:
   4 cups peeled, sliced peaches
4. Mix together in a medium bowl:
   ½ cup rolled oats
   ½ cup packed brown sugar
   ¼ cup whole wheat flour
   ¼ cup canola oil

5. Crumble the oat topping evenly over the sliced fruit. Press it down firmly. Pour evenly over the topping:
   ½ cup orange juice

Peel and thinly slice peaches.

6. Bake for 40 minutes. Let cool to room temperature.

7. Grind mixture in a blender or food processor.

8. See Home-Dried One-Pot Meals in Chapter 1 for dehydrating instructions.

9. Spread food on plastic-covered dehydrator trays and dehydrate for 3½ hours at 145° F.

10. To rehydrate, barely cover with water, boil, stir, and serve.

CAMPING WITH CHILDREN LIST

Backpack Trip with Children

For a backpack trip, take items listed in Backpack List in Chapter 2, plus these extras for a baby:

❑ Child carrier for babies old enough to sit up (can be rented at a camping store)

❑ Hand food grinder

❑ Dehydrated, pureed food

❑ Infant formula

❑ Children's aspirin substitute

❑ Diapers, both cloth and disposable, vinyl or plastic underpants

❑ Ointment

❑ Collapsible bucket for washing cloth diapers

❑ Baby wipes

❑ Washcloths

❑ Bottles, extra nipples

❑ Favorite small toy

❑ Favorite blanket

❑ Extra changes of clothes; keep one set sealed in a plastic bag for emergencies

Backpack Trip with Youngsters

❑ Extra change of clothes in case the child gets thoroughly soaked; keep these clothes sealed in a plastic bag

- ❐ Children's aspirin substitute
- ❐ Simple games and toys
- ❐ Extra snacks

Car Camping with Children

For a car camping trip, take items in the Car Camping List in Chapter 3, plus these extras for a baby:

- ❐ Baby carrier/car seat
- ❐ Child carrier for babies old enough to sit up
- ❐ Hand food grinder
- ❐ Dehydrated, pureed food
- ❐ Infant formula
- ❐ Children's aspirin substitute
- ❐ Diapers, both cloth and disposable, vinyl or plastic underpants
- ❐ Baby wipes
- ❐ Washcloths
- ❐ Ointment
- ❐ Collapsible buckets or other separate, lightweight containers for washing and rinsing cloth diapers

- ❐ Children's aspirin substitute
- ❐ Diapers, both cloth and disposable, vinyl or plastic underpants
- ❐ Baby wipes
- ❐ Ointment
- ❐ Collapsible buckets or other separate, lightweight containers for washing and rinsing cloth diapers
- ❐ Bottles
- ❐ Extra nipples
- ❐ Favorite small toy or blanket

Take these extras for a youngster:

- ❐ Drinking straws to keep drinks from spilling while in vehicle
- ❐ Children's aspirin substitute
- ❐ Box of books, games, and toys
- ❐ Books and songs on tape for vehicle
- ❐ Pillows and blankets for napping in vehicle

Family Favorite Baked Pasta

4 servings

This is a filling meal for children and adults.

1. Cook, then drain in a colander:

   6 ounces capellini or other very thin pasta

2. Preheat oven to 375° F. Oil a 9 by 13-inch glass casserole dish.

3. Beat together in a large bowl:

   2 eggs

   3 cups thick tomato sauce

   8 ounces low-fat ricotta

   ½ cup finely grated Parmesan cheese

   ½ teaspoon sea salt

   ½ teaspoon freshly ground black pepper

Radium Hot Springs,
British Columbia

4. Add the cooked, drained pasta and:
   > 1 bunch fresh spinach, minced
   > 3 cloves garlic, minced
5. Mix well, then pour the pasta mixture into the oiled casserole dish.
6. Bake for 30 minutes.
7. See Home-Dried One-Pot Meals in Chapter 1 for dehydrating instructions.
8. Spread the pasta on plastic-covered dehydrator trays and dehydrate for 5 hours at 145° F.
9. To rehydrate, cover with water, boil, stir, and serve.

No-Bake Oaties

45 cookies

Children age 5 and up can make these high-energy treats at home with minimal supervision. The ingredients are briefly heated on top of the stove, not baked.

1. Bring to a boil in a large skillet over medium heat:
   > ⅔ cup packed brown sugar
   > 2 tablespoons canola oil
   > ⅓ cup water

   Reduce heat and simmer for 2 minutes.
2. Remove from heat and stir in:
   > 1 tablespoon whole wheat flour
   > ¾ cup peanut butter
   > 1 teaspoon vanilla extract
   > 2¼ cups rolled oats
   > ⅓ cup chopped raisins or other chopped dried fruit

¼ cup hulled sunflower
seeds

¼ cup finely chopped wal-
nuts

3. Roll into balls the size of walnuts, set on plates, cover, and
refrigerate until firm. Once
they are firm, they can be stored in plastic bags or
rigid containers at room temperature.

> **While living outdoors, children need snacks more frequently than adults.**

Imaginative Snacks

Our nephew David was a terrific baby backpacker, as long as he was
eating a snack. We handed him thousands of nuts and pretzels, one
at a time. Pack plenty of treats. While living outdoors, children need
snacks more frequently than adults—their blood sugar quickly
becomes depleted, and they need little treats and rewards to keep

Mt. Mansfield, Vermont

going. Keep healthy snacks handy in your pockets and pack and dole them out frequently. When you store your food for the night, be sure to include any snacks you have tucked into your pockets (see Counterbalance Food, Chapter 1).

Make camping snacks more interesting. The same trail mix every day seems boring after a few days. Package individual servings of fruit, nut, candy, and cereal combinations. Try peanuts and chocolate chips, dried apricots and pecans, or dried apples and sunflower seeds.

If you enjoy a variety-filled trail mix, homemade choices are easy and endless. Try creating several different trail mixes for your next trip. Let children combine any or all of the following in individual plastic bags:

- Any variety of shelled nuts
- Shelled sunflower or pumpkin seeds
- Raisins
- Chopped dried fruit
- Shredded coconut
- Popcorn
- Chocolate, carob, or toffee chips
- Grated hard cheese
- Nutritional yeast
- Small pretzels or crackers
- Any ready-to-eat cereal
- Crumbled jerky

Crunchiest Granola

12 cups

1. Heat a large heavy skillet over medium heat. Toast together in the skillet, stirring frequently, until golden:
   1 cup whole wheat flour
   1 cup any other flour, such as soya, barley, buckwheat, or unbleached white

       1 cup wheat germ

       ½ cup sesame seeds

2. Preheat oven to 350° F.

3. Heat gently in a saucepan:

       ¼ cup corn oil

       1 cup peanut butter

       1 cup honey

4. Mix together in a 9 by 13-inch glass casserole dish:

       4½ cups rolled oats

       ½ cup pecans, chopped

       ½ cup hulled sunflower seeds

5. Pour the browned flour mixture and the honey mixture over the oat mixture. Combine thoroughly.

6. Pour evenly over the granola:

       ½ cup any fruit juice

7. Bake for 20 minutes, stir, then bake 20 minutes longer. Turn off the heat and let the granola remain in the oven, with the door closed, for 2 hours.

8. Cool the granola completely, then double-bag it and store in the freezer until ready to use.

9. For camping, package individual servings of granola in 6½-inch square plastic sandwich bags. Place in each bag:

       ⅝ cup Crunchiest Granola

       2 tablespoons instant nonfat dry milk

       2 tablespoons raisins or other chopped, dried fruit

10. To serve, pour ¼–½ cup fresh water into your cup. Add the granola mixture, stir, and enjoy.

Instant Cocoa

1 serving

1. At home, mix together in a small plastic bag:

    3 teaspoons nonfat dry milk

    2 teaspoons packed brown sugar

    1½ teaspoons unsweetened cocoa powder

    6 mini marshmallows

2. In camp, pour a bag full of instant cocoa into a cup. Add while stirring well:

    1 cup boiling water

cocoa

S'Mores

Makes 1 S'More

1. Stack:

    1 square of chocolate candy bar on top of

    1 graham cracker

2. Place firmly on the end of a green stick or a metal skewer:

    1 marshmallow

    Toast the marshmallow over a stove or campfire until it is puffy and golden.

Toast marshmallows.

3. Carefully place the toasted marshmallow on top of the chocolate square.

4. Place on top of the marshmallow:

   1 more graham cracker

5. Wait a minute while the chocolate melts and the marshmallow cools slightly.

6. Enjoy, then make "s'more."

5

PADDLING TRIPS

We heard a soft, whirring sound. Suddenly, 200 silent white pelicans appeared over the lake. Their orange bills and graceful black wing tips caught the late afternoon sun. After circling several times, they descended to the water. We stopped paddling and let our craft glide silently. The regal birds accepted our presence. They gorged on the lake's brine shrimp, tilting back their heads to quickly swallow, then scoop more food.

On the water, you will glimpse scenes of grandeur, quietly view wildlife, admire reflections in mirror-smooth lakes, thrill to exciting river runs, and find a new offshore perspective of the world. Best of all, you'll discover special campsites reachable only by water.

"Yup, you gotta get wet," said the Bureau of Land Management sign at Utah's Escalante River. Whether you're in

> **Take trips that are within your level of comfort and always get yourself and your craft safely out of the water before you become overtired or chilled.**

Personal Flotation Device (PFD)

the water or on it, you must be prepared to get yourself, and your gear, wet. Clothes that shed water and dry fast are essential, as are well-secured, waterproofed equipment and snug-fitting personal flotation devices (PFDs). Whether you're paddling on a lake, drifting down a quiet stream, or running white water, don't consider paddling without a Coast Guard-approved PFD that's designed for paddling. Take trips that are within your level of comfort, and always get yourself and your craft safely out of the water before you become overtired or chilled.

Clothing

While paddling, dress for the water temperature, not the air temperature. On a sunny spring day, the air temperature may be 30 degrees warmer than the water. Unless you're dressed properly in layers, you'll be shivering when you get wet. Start with a lightweight nylon bathing suit worn next to your skin instead of underwear. It is far more comfortable than paddling in soggy cotton drawers. Over the bathing suit, add and remove thin layers of loose, comfortable,

> **On paddling trips, dress for the water temperature, not the air temperature.**

quick-drying clothing as needed. Other layers of clothing can include synthetic long underwear, a neoprene wet suit, breathable nylon shirt and shorts or trousers, and a rain jacket and rain pants.

A day on the river is wonderful fun, but it can leave you wet, cold, and tired—conditions that invite hypothermia. You may be more affected by the cold than you think you are. Assess your condition and that of your companions, and get yourselves warmed up quickly (see Prevent Hypothermia, Chapter 1). Always carry a change of dry clothes and footwear—stored in plastic bags—in your boat. You'll need them later when the evening turns cool. As soon as you stop to set up camp, change into your dry, warm clothes. Take care of your feet immediately. Dry socks and dry camp slippers or athletic shoes are essential to your mental and physical well-being after a day in and on the water. Keep a second sealed bag of dry clothing in your vehicle. If you return wet and tired at the end of your paddling trip, your clean, dry sweat suit, socks, and shoes will feel wonderful.

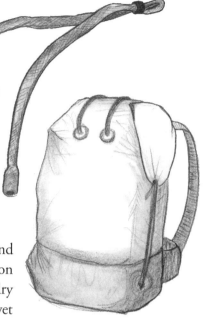

eyeglass retainer

dry bag backpack

When the water temperatures are cold, when you are paddling alone, or when you stand a good chance of capsizing, wear a

> **The best eyeglass retainers for paddling trips are brightly colored and float.**

$\frac{1}{8}$-inch-thick neoprene wet suit for safety and comfort. A layer of synthetic long underwear underneath the wet suit provides extra warmth. Sometimes your feet feel cold while you're paddling, even when the weather is warm. Neoprene socks can keep you comfortable.

Don't lose your eyeglasses or sunglasses. Eyewear should be safely fastened to your head with a retainer. Even if you wear eyeglasses with frames that hook all the way around your ears, secure them with a piece of elastic or a purchased retainer. The best eyeglass retainers for paddling trips are brightly colored and float.

Choose Light, Transportable Gear

Kayaks have limited space for overnight gear. "Dry bags" or your own homemade version fashioned from heavy plastic bags are light and compact, and will squeeze into your kayak more easily than boxes. Use rigid waterproof containers only for breakable, valuable equipment such as cameras or binoculars. Leave heavy, bulky fresh foods at home. Pack dehydrated meals for lighter weight, less bulk, and ease of preparation. (See Home-Dried One-Pot Meals, Chapter 1.) If you are camping in hot summer conditions at low elevations, take a very light, compact sleeping bag. In dry climates, bring your lightest, smallest tent, or simply fashion a shelter from a grommeted tarp and nylon cord. Make sure you bag a dry set of long underwear to use as camp loungewear and pajamas when the evening turns chilly.

When camping with a canoe, raft, or large touring kayak, load as much of your gear into a backpack as possible. You may need to portage unexpectedly, carrying both your gear and your craft. When you must portage around unnavigable rapids, waterfalls, or dams or connect between a chain of lakes, you'll be glad you stowed your gear in a backpack. You may be able to carry everything in just one portage trip instead of three —out, back, and out again. A backpack also lets you camp away from your craft when you wish. Roomy dry bags with shoulder straps and padded waistbelts are available; they serve as ready-made portage backpacks. Alternatively, waterproof your regular backpack (see Keep Gear Dry, below).

Bag gear in 2 plastic bags and 1 or 2 nylon stuff stacks.

Keep Gear Dry

Bag everything in "dry bags," available at camping and boating supply stores, or use the following inexpensive alternative. Buy large, heavy three-mil plastic bags. Place gear that needs to be compacted, such as a tent or a sleeping bag, inside a nylon stuff sack. Then bag it in a three-mil plastic bag. Twist and seal the bag, squeezing out the air. Repeat the process with a second plastic bag. Place the sealed, double plastic bags inside a second heavy nylon stuff sack for abrasion resistance.

Secure Equipment in Boat

I could hear Sarge yelling from shore; her arms waved frantically. We were in trouble. As soon as the canoe tipped, we realized our error. The gear was lashed too loosely. Now it was dangling beneath the overturned canoe and headed toward the bottom of the lake. The dangling dunnage served as a huge anchor, and we skinny scouts couldn't right our craft.

✳ ✳ ✳

Anticipate capsizing. Don't overload your boat. If it's riding too low in the water, you need to leave some of your gear behind. If you can see less than six inches of freeboard, your canoe is overloaded. An overloaded boat will easily capsize.

canoe with lashed gear

Don't sit on your gear or awkwardly stretch around it to paddle; it's both unsafe and likely to cause muscle strain. Make sure all your gear is out of the way of the most sweeping of your paddle or oar strokes. Keep all ropes secured so they can't tangle around your legs if you overturn.

Pack with the weight of your gear kept low, toward the center of the craft, evenly balanced, and out of your way. Center heavy items near the middle of the boat. Pack light gear toward the ends of the boat. If weight is packed unevenly, the boat will list to one side, it will be hard to maneuver, and it will certainly tip more easily. Look at your loaded craft critically before you lash your gear to the boat. Your craft should be trim, riding evenly in the water, both front to back and side to side.

Most important, lash your waterproofed gear securely to the boat. Improperly lashed gear could mean the loss of your valuables and could create long-lasting litter in the lake or river. Use nylon straps with buckles or nylon cord to secure your gear to the boat. Nylon straps are much faster and easier to secure and release than cord. Slip the straps or cord through any available equipment straps or handles, then secure the straps

Secure the bowline.

or the cord to the boat. If you secure your gear with cord, tie quick-release knots.

Keep handy, but secure, the equipment you will need frequently or quickly while you're paddling: map, lunch, drinking water, sunscreen, rain jacket, camera. Some paddlers keep these in a waterproof bag or daypack lashed to the boat. When negotiating white water, you may want to keep these essentials fastened to your body, waterproofed in a fanny pack.

Secure Your Craft on Land

When you're ready to camp for the night, find a landing site with plenty of room. Look for a large area with room to safely bring your boat partway up onto the shore. You'll need space nearby for sleeping, a separate space for cooking, and a toilet area as far away from the water as possible. When you can do so safely, unload your canoe or raft while it's still in the water. This way, you are less likely to scrape the bottom of your boat against the rocky shore. Fasten the bowline and unload your gear. Then gently move your craft well up onto shore. Finally, be sure the bowline is hitched securely to a boulder or tree, in case the water level and winds rise during the night. Don't let your boat get away from you.

Hitch your boat.

> Be sure the bowline is hitched securely to a boulder or tree in case the water level and winds rise during the night.

Shakedown Cruise

A camping trip utilizing a canoe, kayak, or raft will be a pleasant surprise. On a trip without portages, paddling is far less strenuous than backpacking. You can travel in comfort toting a heavier, bulkier load of gear. From the water, the unique view of the landscape and wildlife and the silent beauty that cannot be seen except by paddling will make you an instant convert. You may be so enthused you'll make boating the centerpiece of more of your holidays.

Before heading off to Labrador for a month-long, portage-filled wilderness river experience, try some shakedown cruises near home. Rent or borrow a canoe or kayak and a snug-fitting personal flotation device. Take a training course or ask experienced friends to accompany you. Experiment with your craft. Learn how to overturn the boat and recover it before attempting a camping trip with a loaded boat.

> **River maps detail put-in and take-out points and campsites, and they rate stretches of river for difficulty from Class I to Class VI.**

Try an easy one-night trip on a lake or quiet river. This will be an opportunity to hone your water camping skills. First waterproof your gear, then load your craft evenly, and finally lash the gear securely to the boat. Even if you have paddled the same boat for years, it will ride differently when it is loaded with overnight gear. Learn how to control your boat while on an easy weekend trip.

Avoid aching arms and back and blisters on your palms. Don't paddle for too many hours at a time. Protect your hands with deerskin, polypropylene, heavy household rubber, or neoprene gloves. If you're making an out-and-back trip, don't go too far on the outward leg. You should feel fresh, not exhausted, when you begin the return trip. A tired paddler can make dangerous errors in judgment.

River guidebooks are available for hundreds of the world's rivers. If a guidebook isn't available for your river, look for a river map. River maps detail put-in and take-out points and campsites, and they rate stretches of river for difficulty from Class I through Class VI. If neither a river guidebook nor a river map is available, rely on a topo map (see Maps, Chapter 2). Study your map before you go, then continually compare it to the actual topography. If you pack your map inside a dry bag along with all your other equipment, you won't bother using it. Keep your map handy and protected while paddling. Place it inside a waterproof map case, or double-bag it in one-gallon size zip-top bags, and fasten it to your craft with duct tape. Your map needs to be right in front of you at all times.

Well before your trip, learn about public access to your chosen watercourse. Obtain permits if needed for camping, river, or lake use. Popular national parks require permits, often reserved well in advance, for each campsite.

Keep in mind that water attracts insects. Pack plenty of insect repellent and keep your skin covered with trousers, a long-sleeved shirt, a hat, and a mosquito head net if necessary. It's difficult to swat mosquitoes while you're paddling.

At Home in and on the Water

Know how to bob, float, and swim well. Be confident in the water, not fearful. Learn standard paddling strokes while in a safe situation. Be able to execute the basic strokes and maneuver the boat automatically. Deliberately capsize your boat and recover it in a safe situation with helpers ready to come to your aid. More people accidentally fall into the water two feet from shore while entering their boats than while underway, so concentrate while entering and exiting your craft. Keep low, toward the center of the boat, and move slowly.

> **More people accidentally fall into the water two feet from shore while entering their boats than while underway, so concentrate while entering and exiting your craft.**

Learn to recognize the signs of approaching weather (see Weather, Chapter 4, and Lightning, Chapter 1). You don't want to be caught paddling your craft in the center of a large lake when a thunderstorm strikes. Pay attention to wind direction. If you have to paddle back to camp into a strong wind, you could become exhausted. Since the wind usually builds up during the afternoon, paddle early on days when strong winds seem likely. Always plan for rain. A tent can be a real lifesaver on a paddling trip.

> **Since the wind usually builds up during the afternoon, paddle early on days when strong winds seem likely.**

Early in the year, when springtime rivers run high and very cold, use special caution. If you overturn into freezing water, you'll need to get out immediately. Don't paddle solo. You may need help getting out of icy, swift waters. Your PFD can keep you afloat, but it can't prevent hypothermia. You can be safer and more comfortable if you wear a neoprene wet suit under your PFD whenever you paddle very cold waters. Layer synthetic long underwear underneath the wet suit for extra protection from the cold.

Plan Campsites Ahead of Time

Before you leave home, obtain a river guidebook, river map, or topo map for your river and study it, mile by mile. Look for good campsites: roomy, high, dry, and airy, away from the water, with a good landing site, and maybe even a spectacular view. Avoid low, swampy, buggy areas and rocky shorelines. Camp away from the river whenever you can. You will cause less damage to the environment and be more comfortable away from waterborne winds and insects and gritty beach sand that seems to stick to everything. When you must camp on a sandy or pebbly beach, staking your tent will require extra effort. You can carry specialized

sand stake for a tent

triangular sand stakes. These stakes are large and heavy, but effective in sand or pebbles.

Since regular thin, straight stakes are designed for use in soil, not sand, they need extra support when used on beaches. If you pack regular stakes, weight them with heavy rocks placed directly on top of the stakes, or placed on the guylines (brace lines) between the tent and the stakes. You can eliminate stakes entirely if you secure your tent by tying the lines directly to heavy rocks; place several additional rocks around the main rock to prevent slippage. When you break camp, be sure to replace any rocks you have moved.

> **Tie padding to the tops of the supporting branches to keep them from puncturing the tarp.**

On lightweight trips in dry, warm climates, fashion a shelter from a grommeted tarp and nylon cord and leave your tent at home. Use a tarp with six or more grommets (metal or unbreakable plastic eyelets) around its edges. Many tarps are manufactured with grommets. Alternatively, purchase a grommet kit; insert the grommets in the corners and along the sides of your existing tarp. A versatile grommeted tarp can be used as a shelter and also can be lashed down to protect gear on your back or in your boat or motor vehicle. Insert nylon cord through the grommets. Staked to form just a roof, the tarp will provide shade on exposed beaches and let the afternoon breeze cool you. When the evening becomes chilly, stake the tarp's sides lower. Use nylon cord and rocks to stake the corners of your tarp. If no trees or large shrubs are available, support the center or corners of your tarp

Tie tent lines to heavy rocks.

with branches or paddles stuck in the sand. Tie padding to the tops of the supporting branches to keep them from puncturing the tarp.

> **Buy or rent personal flotation devices designed for young children complete with leg straps to keep children from sliding out.**

Search the topo maps and river guide for exploration opportunities as well as possible campsites. You can use your boat to gain access to otherwise unreachable country, then make a base camp. Find a good beach or meadow in the vicinity of an interesting-looking side canyon, and camp for several nights while exploring the side canyon and perhaps a nearby peak on foot. Time spent hiking loosens muscles made stiff by paddling. It's a welcome diversion.

Plan campsites and alternate sites in advance. Estimate the number of miles you might paddle each day. Ten to fifteen gentle miles, with plenty of rest stops, will be comfortable for most beginners. The actual miles paddled each day will vary widely, so mark plenty of contingency campsites on your map. Be conservative. Don't be caught too long in steep river canyons without banks or beaches for camping. Stop early—there is no turning back on a swiftly flowing river.

Paddling with Children

For children who are reluctant hikers, a paddling trip on gentle waters will be a pleasure for the whole family (see Chapter 4, Camping with Children). While on a paddling trip, don't keep active children confined in a boat for too many hours. Choose an easy first trip. Paddle across a lake, or a short distance down a quiet river, to a secluded campsite. In camp, the children can swim, splash, or fish. Watch children closely at all times while in or around water. Adults and children alike need to wear their PFDs while they are near the water as well as while they are on it or in it.

PADDLING LIST

Take items listed in Backpack List, Chapter 2, plus:

Boat and Accessories

☐ Boat

    ☐ Paddle(s) or oars

    ☐ extra paddle, secured to craft

☐ Nylon rope for rescue and for securing gear to boat

☐ Nylon cord or buckled nylon webbing to secure gear to boat

☐ Throwbag. This is a foam block with an attached floating rope, for rescue of boaters and craft. The bag design keeps the rope from tangling around your legs when you tip.

☐ Waterproof bags. Buy "dry bags," tapered models that fit your kayak or canoe, or make your own (see Keep Gear Dry, this chapter).

☐ Waterproof boxes or buckets, made of plastic, with tight-sealing lids, are available used from restaurants, or use army surplus ammunition cans.

☐ Waterproof camera case

☐ Bailer. At home, fill a one-gallon screw-top plastic jug with hot water. Let it stand for 5 minutes, then drain the jug. Cut off the bottom of the jug with a sharp knife; cut on a slant, forming a large, deep scoop. Fasten the screw-top tightly to the jug. Tie the bailer to your boat with a piece of nylon cord tied to the jug's handle.

bailer

Boat Repair

☐ 2-inch-wide silver duct tape or boat repair tape

PADDLING LIST (CONTINUED)

- Pocket tool kit that includes pliers and screwdrivers
- Patching kit for inflatable boats that includes glue and patch material

Clothing

- Personal flotation device (PFD), Coast Guard-approved, designed for paddling

- Helmet, if paddling a kayak, or in any white water. Get one that protects your temples, forehead, ears, and the sides and back of your head.
- Neoprene or rubber gloves for cold weather, or lightweight deerskin or synthetic gloves to prevent blisters in warm weather
- Neoprene socks
- Neoprene wet suit, ⅛-inch thick

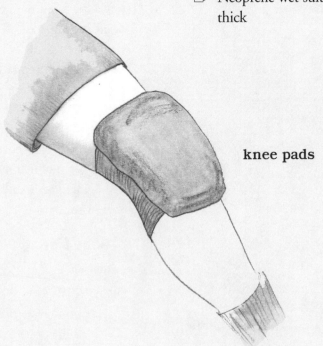

knee pads

PADDLING LIST (CONTINUED)

❑ Knee pads for canoeing, portable type that wraps around knees, or use barge cement to glue pieces of closed-cell foam to canoe

❑ Thick-soled neoprene shoes or boots, or nylon athletic shoes or boots. Footwear should protect your toes and must be well secured to your feet and not come loose if you wade through mud.

❑ Extra changes of quick-drying synthetic clothing

❑ Extra set of synthetic long underwear

❑ Extra pair of shoes for camp wear and hiking; keep them dry in a plastic bag

❑ Extra pair of socks for camp wear and hiking; keep them dry in plastic bag

❑ Straps for eyeglasses/sunglasses

Food, Water, and Shelter

❑ Portable stove

❑ Fuel for the stove

or

❑ Fire pan and metal fire box—may be required for campfires on popular rivers. Buy a fire pan or use a metal garbage can lid, a barbecue, or a hubcap. Carry charcoal if firewood will not be available. Take a cooking grill to hold your pot over the campfire.

❑ Candle as emergency fire starter

❑ Large sponges for wiping equipment and boat

❑ Grommeted tarp and extra nylon cord to create a roof in your kitchen area, or shade your sitting area on exposed beaches

❑ Portable latrine (may be required on popular rivers). Inquire when you obtain permits. Available from rafting supply stores.

All members of the party, especially babies and young children, need PFDs that fit. Buy or rent PFDs designed for young children with leg straps that keep them from sliding out.

- Train everyone in capsize procedures while in a safe, warm-water setting.
- Teach children to swim, and especially to tread water and float, before you take them on a paddling trip.
- Test the fit and effectiveness of your children's PFDs. Fasten the PFD on your child and have her float limp and relaxed in a pool. The PFD should completely support your child and keep her face well out of the water. You and your child will feel secure knowing that the PFD completely supports her.

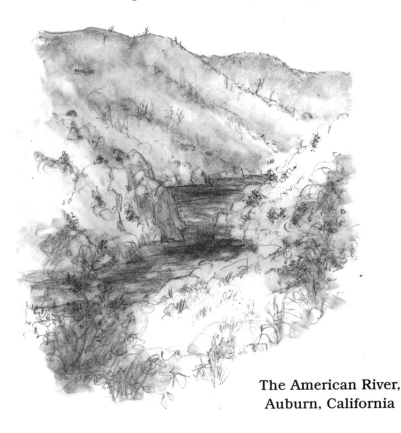

**The American River,
Auburn, California**

While in, on, or near water, plan a high ratio of adults to children, preferably one to one, for safety. Don't take children on water whose conditions are rated higher than Class I (Easy). Before you take children on a paddling trip, be experienced and comfortable in the water yourself. Teach your children to be relaxed and respectful around water, not fearful.

Duct Tape

duct tape

Don't forget to carry duct tape, or boat repair tape, for all your emergency repairs. A large roll of silver duct tape will repair almost any damage to your craft or other torn, broken, or punctured equipment. Wipe dry the damaged part of your craft. Set it in direct sunlight. The damaged area needs to be as warm and dry as possible before you apply the tape. Firmly apply generous lengths of duct tape. If you can refloat your craft successfully, permanent repairs can wait until you reach your take-out point.

> A large roll of silver duct tape will repair almost any damage to your craft or other torn, broken, or punctured equipment.

Paddling Kitchen

Prior to your overnight or multiday paddling trip, plan your menu (see Menu Plan, Chapter 2). Your menu plan depends on how much room you have on your craft(s), how much weight you can comfortably take on board, and how much time you want to devote to food preparation while camping. Do you want to cook in the field, or simply heat foods while you're camping? Will you carry a portable stove and fuel, or will you cook over a campfire? If you plan to build campfires, you'll need to carry a fire pan. If firewood isn't available, you'll need to bring charcoal briquettes. Check the campfire regulations for your chosen area.

For a lightweight, low-bulk trip, lasting one or two weeks, emphasize dried foods (see Home-Dried One-Pot Meals, Chapter 1). Cook and dehydrate your hot meals at home, then quickly reheat them in the field using a portable stove. A lightweight paddling trip menu will resemble a backpack menu.

When your route will not require portages, and you have room on your craft for more weight and bulk, you can enjoy some fresh foods, such as fruits and salads. If you are planning a short, portage-free trip and your craft is a touring canoe or kayak or a full-sized raft, you can carry a larger, heavier portable kitchen.

Using a cast-iron or cast-aluminum Dutch oven and a wood or charcoal fire, you can cook, and even bake, many of the dishes you prepare at home (see Quick-to-Prepare Foods That Store Well in Chapter 3). Be sure to carry a metal fire pan and a fire box to protect delicate river environments and contain the fire's ashes. You can improvise a fire pan by using a metal garbage can lid or a metal hubcap. If permissible, you can build a wood fire in your fire pan; when burning downed wood is not permitted, or wood is not available, carry charcoal briquettes for your fire pan campfires. Set your fire pan on rocks to avoid scorching the soil, sand, and plants. Place a little dirt, sand, or ashes from your previous fire in the bottom of the pan to prevent burning through the metal. Use a metal grill to hold your pot.

The next day, pack out the campfire's ashes in a fireproof metal box or dispose of them properly. Before your trip, learn the land management agency's rules for disposal. Do not leave the remains of any fire at your riverside campsite.

When preparing fresh foods in the field, guard against food spoilage and foodborne illness. Store your perishable foods, along with frozen jugs of water, in ice chests (see Ice Chest, Chapter 3). For paddling, choose a heavy-duty ice chest that clamps shut. Seal the ice chest shut with duct tape, then secure it to your boat with nylon buckles or cord. Keep perishable foods on ice, and use them as soon as possible. Perishables include protein foods such as meat, eggs, soft cheese, milk, and cooked beans. Later in your trip, you can use other, less-perishable, fresh foods, such as quick-cooking grains, vegetables, hard cheese, and dried beans.

As you write your menu plan, remember that you will become very hungry on a paddling trip and will need plenty of fats and sugars, especially in cold air or cold water temperatures. Prevent hypothermia by including plenty of sugary snacks and sweet, hot drinks in your menu, such as hot cups of cocoa (see Instant Cocoa, Chapter 4).

Don't depend upon freshly caught fish as part of your menu plan. Bring all of the food you need from home. If you enjoy fishing, carry a telescoping rod and fish for pleasure on your paddling adventures. When you are fortunate enough to catch some fish, and you're able to use a wood or charcoal campfire, the following is the simplest way to prepare trout or any small fish. You don't even need a frying pan.

Grilled Trout

Allow 1 or more fish per serving.

1. Let your wood or charcoal campfire burn down to hot coals.
2. Lay directly on the hot coals:
   Whole, gutted trout; leave skin intact
3. Cook for 3 minutes, then turn and cook 3 minutes longer.

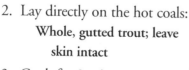

rainbow trout

Here are some easy dinners to dehydrate at home and enjoy while paddling.

Marcia's Broadway Chili

4 servings

1. Cook:

   1 cup dried pinto beans, or use 2½ cups canned beans

   Drain the beans. Reserve the bean liquid.

2. Heat a cast-iron Dutch oven over medium heat, then add:

   2 tablespoons olive oil

   When the oil is hot, add and cook, stirring, until lightly browned:

   2 onions, finely chopped

   3 cloves garlic, minced

   1 green bell pepper, finely chopped

3. Add and cook a few minutes longer:

   2 tablespoons ground cumin

   ¼ teaspoon ground cinnamon

   ¼ teaspoon ground cloves

   ¼ teaspoon ground allspice

   2 teaspoons fresh oregano, minced, or 1 teaspoon dried

4. Add the reserved cooked beans and:

   1 (28-ounce) can chopped tomatoes, including liquid

   1 teaspoon honey

   1 teaspoon sea salt

   2 tablespoons chili powder

   4 jalapeño peppers, fresh or canned, seeded and minced

¼ cup chopped fresh parsley

1 cup bean liquid or any variety stock

⅓ cup polenta (coarse cornmeal)

5. Simmer for 45 minutes, or until thick.

6. See Home-Dried One-Pot Meals, Chapter 1, for dehydrating instructions.

7. Spread chili on plastic-covered dehydrator trays and dehydrate for 5 hours at 145° F.

8. To rehydrate, cover with water, boil, stir, and serve with Crispy Crackers (see Chapter 7) or Peanut Chapatis (see Chapter 2).

Shrimp and Corn Chowder

4 servings

1. Heat a cast-iron Dutch oven over medium heat. Add:

    2 tablespoons olive oil

    When the oil is hot, add:

    1 large onion, minced

    Sauté the onion for 2 minutes, stirring frequently, then add:

    2 medium-sized russet potatoes, scrubbed but not peeled, minced

    Reduce heat and cook for 20 minutes, or until brown.

Use fresh shrimp.

2. Add:

    4 cups any variety stock

    Salt and freshly ground black pepper to taste

    Cover, bring to a boil, reduce heat, and simmer for 10 minutes.

3. Add, bring to a boil, then simmer for 3 minutes:

    1 pound fresh shrimp, shelled and chopped

    1½ cups whole corn kernels

    1 teaspoon minced fresh basil or ½ teaspoon dried

4. Add and reheat gently:

    1 cup nonfat milk

5. Remove from heat and stir in:

    ¼ cup finely grated Parmesan cheese

6. See Home-Dried One-Pot Meals, Chapter 1, for dehydrating instructions.

7. Spread chowder on plastic-covered dehydrator trays and dehydrate for 5½ hours at 145° F.

8. To rehydrate, cover with water, boil, stir, and serve with Crispy Crackers (see Chapter 7) or Peanut Chapatis (see Chapter 2).

Vegetable Crunch

4 servings

1. Heat a large, ovenproof skillet or Dutch oven over medium heat. Add:

    2 tablespoons corn oil

    When the oil is hot, add:

    1 onion, finely chopped

    Cook, stirring, for 3 minutes, then add:

    1 pound tofu or ground turkey, crumbled

    1 carrot, finely chopped

    10 mushrooms, finely chopped

2. Cook, stirring occasionally, for 5 minutes, then reduce heat to low and add:

    2 cups chopped tomatoes, fresh or canned

    6 ounces tomato paste

    2 cups finely chopped broccoli

    4 cloves garlic, minced

    1 teaspoon fresh sage, minced, or ½ teaspoon dried, crumbled

    ¼ teaspoon cayenne pepper

    ¼ teaspoon sea salt

Cover and simmer for 10 minutes.

3. Preheat oven to 400° F.

4. Mix together in a medium bowl:

    ½ cup pecans, finely chopped

    ½ cup whole wheat flour

    ½ cup finely grated Parmesan or dry Monterey Jack cheese

    ¼ cup rolled oats

Stir in:

    ¼ cup corn oil

5. Sprinkle the nut mixture over the vegetables in the skillet. Bake for 30 minutes, or until browned.

6. See Home-Dried One-Pot Meals, Chapter 1, for dehydrating instructions.

7. Spread the Vegetable Crunch on plastic-covered dehydrator trays and dehydrate for 4½ hours at 145° F.

8. To rehydrate, cover with water, boil, stir, and serve.

Biscotti

42 slices

These slightly sweet Italian biscuits will keep for weeks.

1. Preheat oven to 375° F. Oil a large baking sheet.

2. Beat together in a medium bowl:

    ⅓ cup corn oil

¾ cup packed brown sugar

2 whole eggs plus 2 egg whites

2 teaspoons vanilla extract

3. Stir in:

1 cup whole wheat flour

1 cup unbleached white flour

2 teaspoons baking powder

1½ cups any variety nuts, finely chopped

Blend thoroughly.

4. Divide dough in half. Shape each portion into a 10-inch log. Place logs on oiled baking sheet and bake for 20 minutes or until golden brown.

5. Remove from oven and let cool on the baking sheet for 1 hour.

6. Preheat oven to 350° F. Cut logs diagonally into ½-inch-thick slices. Place slices on their sides on ungreased baking sheets and bake for 10 minutes. Turn the slices over and bake them 5 minutes longer, or until crisp and lightly browned.

7. Let cool thoroughly, then store in an airtight container.

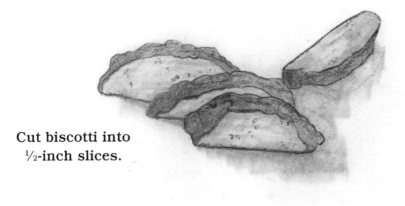

Cut biscotti into ½-inch slices.

6

WINTER CAMPING

It's cold. You feel stiff and clumsy pushing off on your skis, your heavy backpack shifting into place as you ski away from your vehicle into the forest. Half an hour later, you're warm. Your eyes are sparkling, your face glowing. Your pack has settled comfortably. You're moving rhythmically. Now you're comfortable enough to enjoy your surroundings: blue sky, snow-laden evergreens, dark, mysterious creeks, and animal tracks in the fresh snow. Most of all you notice the silence, broken only by the soft whoosh of your skis, muffled by the snow. Suddenly the forest opens up. Before you, a bowl of fresh, firm snow stretches invitingly.

✳ ✳ ✳

Enjoy winter intimately—the quietest and most beautiful season—while camping. You will have the backcountry to yourself, and will witness the splendor of winter sunsets and sunrises. This special time of year is also the most unforgiving, so planning is more essential than ever.

Before your trip, gather information. Contact the U.S. Forest Service; national, state, or provincial park; wilderness area; and any local ski clubs in your area of choice. Ask about snow conditions, terrain, required permits, and camping possibilities. Will there be snow? How deep? What kind of snow? Are there campsites near unfrozen streams, so you won't have to melt all your drinking water? Ask if huts are available; if they are, you could enjoy an especially comfortable snow-touring trip. Reserve hut space in advance and ski or snowshoe between several indoor lodgings, or use one hut as a base camp.

Weather conditions will dictate your choice of winter camping equipment. You can backpack wearing hiking boots on shallow, hard-packed snow, using instep crampons and an ice axe over slippery areas. If two or more feet of snow cover the ground, you'll need snowshoes, or cross-country skis and poles. Winter camping in milder areas of North America means being prepared for cold, heavy rains. Wherever you go in winter, keep a close watch on the weather.

Avoid early winter or midwinter snow camping trips. Days are cold and depressingly short. Too many long nighttime hours in your tent will make you feel stiff in the morning. In late winter and early spring, warmer longer days are more cheerful and comfortable. Spring skiing on a warm sunny morning, when the snow is still firm, is heavenly.

touring skis

Group Travel

> **Plan to cover very little distance every day.**

Four or more people traveling together form a safely sized winter camping party. If someone is injured, one person can stay with the injured camper, while the

The following books read well on camping trips. They are all available in paperback.

Abbey, Edward. *Desert Solitaire: A Season in the Wilderness.* New York: Ballantine, 1985.

Austin, Mary. *Land of Little Rain.* Albuquerque, NM: University of New Mexico Press, 1974.

Cherry-Garrard, Apsley. *The Worst Journey in the World.* New York: Carroll & Graf, 1997. (Cherry-Garrard was a surviving member of Scott's Antarctic party. Cherry-Garrard's neighbor at home in England, George Bernard Shaw, is said to have suggested the book's title.)

Conrad, Joseph; Samuel Hynes, Ed. *The Collected Stories of Joseph Conrad.* Hopewell, NJ: Ecco Press, 1996.

Duncan, David James. *The River Why.* New York: Bantam Doubleday Dell, 1988.

Fletcher, Colin. *The Man Who Walked Through Time.* New York: Vintage Books, 1989.

Herzog, Maurice. *Annapurna: First Conquest of an 8,000-Meter Peak.* New York: Lyons Press, 1997.

Jerome, Jerome K. *Three Men in a Boat: Three Men on the Bummel.* New York: Viking Penguin, 1978.

McPhee, John. *Coming into the Country.* New York: Noonday Press, 1991.

Morris, Jan. *Destinations: Essays from Rolling Stone.* New York: Oxford University Press, 1982.

Mowat, Farley. *Never Cry Wolf.* New York: Bantam Books, 1983.

Muir, John. *My First Summer in the Sierra.* New York: Viking Penguin, 1987.

Scott, Robert Falcon. *Scott's Last Expedition: The Journals.* New York: Carroll & Graf, 1996. (Scott's own story of his attainment of, and attempted return from, the

Winter Reading List (continued)

South Pole in 1912.)

Stegner, Wallace. *Beyond the Hundredth Meridian: John Wesley Powell and the Second Opening of the West.* New York: Viking Penguin, 1992.

Theroux, Paul. *To the Ends of the Earth: The Selected Travels of Paul Theroux.* New York: Ivy Books, 1994.

Thoreau, Henry David. *Walden, or Life in the Woods and Civil Disobedience.* New York: NAL/Dutton, 1976.

Twain, Mark. *Roughing It.* New York: Hippocrene Books, 1988.

Wallace, David Rains. *The Klamath Knot.* San Francisco: Sierra Club Books, 1984.

Williams, Terry Tempest. *Refuge: An Unnatural History of Family and Place.* New York: Vintage Books, 1992.

other two seek help. Try to stay within sight and sound of each other at all times. Wear bright colors.

Traveling in a group gives the party the combined knowledge of all of its members. Decisions are best made jointly, but if one of you has winter camping experience, let the experienced person have the final say. During most of the trip, the strongest, most experienced members of the party can lead and break trail for the others. This exhilarating job requires concentration and physical strength, but be sure to trade so each member of the party has the thrill of leading some of the time.

Winter touring while wearing a heavy backpack is extraordinarily tiring work. Plan to cover very little distance per day. You may cover only one mile of dis-

> **Don't let your rest breaks last too long. If you get too cold, your body will stiffen up.**

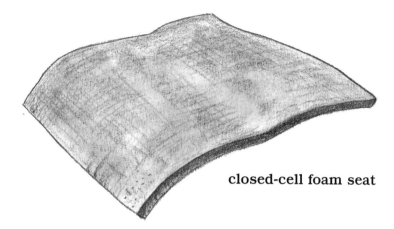

closed-cell foam seat

tance every two hours while breaking trail and route-finding over rugged terrain.

Constantly monitor yourself and your companions for signs of cold-induced problems. You may not recognize that the cold is adversely affecting you, yet you will notice that a companion is stumbling, lagging behind, or displaying poor judgment. Stop and take care of yourself and your companions (see Prevent Hypothermia, Chapter 1).

Take rest stops for 10 minutes once an hour, just as you would during a backpack trip. Break even more frequently in rugged terrain. Make sure the weakest member of your party remains fresh. Don't let your rest breaks last too long. If you let yourself get stiff and chilled, it's difficult to get moving again.

I like to keep a small closed-cell foam pad handy. Strap one to the outside of your pack. Use it as a comfortable seat on the snow during rest breaks.

A group base camp makes winter camping easier. After snow touring during the day, you can return to your already-prepared camp. Camp chores take a little longer in winter than in summer. A group working together makes the chores go faster. When you leave your group base camp for day touring, either keep the group together, within sight of each other, or equip each person with the following essentials. Each group of people traveling together or each person traveling solo must carry these basics in addition to their warm clothing.

- Map
- Whistle
- Compass

- Knife
- Waterproof match safe

Prevent Frostbite

Skin exposed to extreme cold can freeze. In very cold, windy conditions, prevent frostbite by sheltering in your tent. Keep bare skin covered. Protect your vulnerable extremities. Don't remove your gloves, even when it's frustrating to perform chores with gloves on. Cover your nose, cheeks, and ears with a balaclava or face mask. A balaclava is a knit hat that can be rolled down to cover your face or rolled up to protect just your head. Monitor yourself and your companions for the early signs of frostbite. First skin turns very red, then progresses to gray, then becomes white as the condition worsens. Frostbitten skin feels numb, stiff, and hard. Gently and gradually warm the affected areas. Do not rub. Seek medical attention as soon as possible.

> **After an energetic day in the snow, your body cools down unbelievably fast when you stop at night.**

Cold Weather Clothing

Puffing uphill on touring skis, wearing your backpack, will make you perspire, even on an overcast, subzero-degree day. Later, while standing around camp, you'll be stamping your feet, trying to stay warm. After an energetic day in the snow, your body cools down unbelievably fast when you stop at night. Do you feel too warm or too cold? Adjust your clothing immediately. Don't let your cloth-

Take advantage of sun and wind at your campsite to dry out wet gear.

ing become perspiration-soaked during the day. Wet clothing will make you feel chilled later on. While on the move, I like to keep extra layers of clothing handy, tied around my waist, for quick changes. A fleece jacket might feel too warm while you're exercising, but it's perfect to wear around your waist and slip on when you stop for a rest break.

Keep your clothing and all of your equipment as dry as possible. While camping in winter conditions, you will always have some damp clothing and equipment. Clothing becomes damp as it absorbs your perspiration. Your sleeping bag and tent become damp during the night from your respira-

synthetic T-shirt

wool or synthetic sweater

waterproof and windproof jacket

tion. Melted snow soaks through your boots and socks. Try to dry your clothes and equipment whenever you can. Take advantage of sun and wind at your campsite to dry out wet gear. While you are moving from one campsite to another, use your backpack as a laundry line. Attach damp clothes to your pack and let them flap dry.

Cold weather camping requires three basic layers of clothing—and constant adjustment of these layers. In very cold conditions you will need several additional layers, but these three basics are the minimum standard for cold weather comfort.

- *The layer next to your skin*, such as a breathable synthetic T-shirt, will wick moisture away from your skin, so you don't feel either chilled or overly warm.
- *The middle layer*, such as a wool or synthetic shirt or sweater, keeps you warm. Keep this layer dry. Protect it from moisture from your body and from the atmosphere.
- *The outer layer*, which must be waterproof and windproof, but breathable, keeps you dry.

Take plenty of clothing when camping during the winter. A few extra layers, such as a second windbreaker and an additional turtleneck, are well worth their slight extra weight. A person who feels cold in a drafty room at home will feel very cold in low temperatures and high winds while living outdoors during the winter. You can feel comfortable outdoors in winter conditions—if you are wearing enough layers of clothing.

Large, secure pockets with zipper, snap, or hook-and-loop closures are a welcome feature in all winter clothing. So are full-length zippers on jackets and side zippers on wind pants. When choosing winter camping clothes, look for features that make the clothing easier to add or remove, such as a roomy design or an elasticized waistband. Put large, easy-to-grip pulls on all your zippers so they're easy to manipulate when you're wearing gloves (see Zippers, Chapter 2).

Footwear

In between backcountry trips, clean your leather boots carefully to remove dirt, mud, and grease. After cleaning, let them dry slowly, away from all heat sources. Finally, apply wax-based waterproofing sealant. Even the most carefully waterproofed boots will get wet during winter camping trips. Well-cared-for boots will dry quite well overnight while camping if you bag them and keep them inside the foot of your sleeping bag (see Take Your Boots to Bed in this chapter).

> **When your feet are cold, you feel cold all over.**

Take extra socks. At all times, you must have at least one dry pair ready to put on. Dry damp socks overnight inside your sleeping bag, or pin them to your backpack to dry in the sun and wind during the day.

When your feet are cold, you feel cold all over. Cold feet can be downright painful and even dangerous. During the day, while you're on the move, keep your feet warm by wicking away moisture with liner socks, covered by thick wool or synthetic outer socks. At the end of a day of exercise, don't let your feet get chilled. Remove your wet boots and socks immediately. Change into dry socks. In camp, wear dry socks and athletic shoes, or down or synthetic-filled booties combined with waterproof cloth overboots that will keep your booties dry while you're walking around camp.

Gloves and Mittens

You'll need thin liner gloves whenever you are outside in cold weather. Over these, wear heavy, waterproof mittens or gloves. You'll frequently need to remove your heavy gloves while using your camera, rummaging through your pack, setting up camp, or heating food and melting snow. Meanwhile, you will need to keep your heavy mittens or gloves handy and dry. Remember the elastic strap with clips that kept you from losing your mittens as a child? Create one from cord or heavy elastic. Run the cord up one

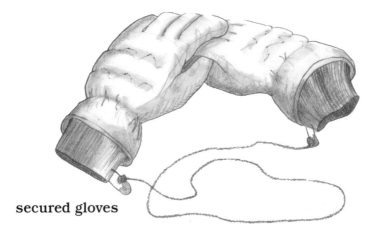

secured gloves

sleeve of your shirt or jacket, across your back, and down the other sleeve. Using diaper pins or the clips on your gloves, fasten your heavy mittens or gloves to the ends of the cord.

Large-Capacity Winter Backpack

Winter camping requires a large-capacity backpack. You must carry more clothing, and more food, than during warm weather. You will need a shovel or a sturdy trowel. While snow camping, you must carry additional stove fuel for heating plenty of hot drinks and soups and for melting snow for your drinking water. All of this equipment will not fit into a summer-sized backpack. You could borrow, rent, or buy a very large backpack; an oversized pack can be used for warm-weather backpack trips, too. Look for a winter backpack with a 6,000- or 7,000-cubic-inch capacity. Choose an internal frame pack with ski slots or holsters; you will sometimes want to carry your skis on your back.

If you carry your regular backpack in winter conditions, you'll need to give it additional capacity. Load your excess equipment into nylon stuff sacks and strap the sacks securely to your pack. The volume of gear will be reduced each day as you eat the food you're carrying.

Balance is key when skiing or snowshoeing while carrying a heavy backpack. Keep the right and left sides of your pack equal in weight. Load your backpack with the heaviest items low and close to your back. You will need to carry the weight lower than for summer camping because weight and stability on snow are needed near your hips, not up around your shoulders. Internal frame backpacks are best for skiing and snowshoeing because the pack's weight is held lower and closer to your back. Weight carried high can cause skiers and snowshoers to fall more easily. An occasional fall is part of skiing; repeated falls while wearing a backpack are tiring.

> Winter camping requires a large-capacity backpack. You must carry more clothing and more food than during warm weather.

Winter Campsite

Look for a campsite not far from a running, unfrozen stream. Whenever you can, avoid melting snow for all your water needs. Melting snow is time-consuming. It requires a lot of fuel.

Take time to find campsites that are as safe as possible from avalanches. You may remain in the same camp for days, either by choice or if you are kept in your tent by a snowstorm, so choose your site carefully. Before your trip, check with

> Load your backpack with the heaviest items low and close to your back. You will need to carry the weight lower than for summer camping because weight and stability on snow are needed near your hips, not up around your shoulders.

rangers about avalanche conditions. Local authorities can also warn you about areas with high winds or other hazards. Avoid skiing or camping below steep, narrow chutes, or any steep slopes that could possibly avalanche. Evaluate the slopes in all directions. A large avalanche on one side of a valley can cross the valley and come partway up the opposite slope.

If you are caught unexpectedly by a storm, quickly choose a safe location, set up your tent, and wait it out.

Be especially careful during or just after a snowfall. This is the time when most avalanches occur. When a big storm seems imminent, plan to pack out quickly, or make a snug, safe camp and be prepared to wait as long as you need to. Take an absorbing paperback book and plenty of extra flashlight batteries. Make sure you have all of your gear either inside the tent or in the tent's vestibule. If you must leave some of your equipment outside, bag it in plastic and tie it with nylon cord. Choose a sheltered location for the gear you need to leave outside, and know exactly where to find it. Avoid traveling in the backcountry while it is actually snowing. If you are caught unexpectedly by a storm, quickly choose a safe location, set up your tent, and wait it out. Traveling in whiteout blizzard conditions can be extremely dangerous. You could fall off a precipice or wander in circles, cold and hungry.

Look for campsites located below very gentle slopes, those with less than 30 degrees of steepness. Large boulders and brush or trees on the slopes above you are good signs; these features help hold the snow and prevent it from avalanching. Avoid cold valleys. Look for higher, open areas, free from dead or snow-laden tree branches. Site your tent with the entrance pointed downhill, away from cold winds blowing down off the peaks.

Site your tent with the entrance pointed downhill, away from cold winds blowing down off the peaks.

When you've found a campsite, first prepare a sleeping area. While wearing your skis or snowshoes, firmly stamp out a level tent area, including a "patio" for putting on boots, just outside your tent's entrance. Scoop out slight depressions in the snow for your hips and shoulders. Spread your ground cloth on the snow, lie down, and fit the depressions to your body. Using your shovel, create windbreaks, seating, and cooking areas from blocks of snow. Let your tent area and your other constructions sit for half an hour before using them. This waiting period gives the snow time to firm up. When you break camp, knock down any counters or walls you have created. Try to leave no trace. Keep the chores of setting up camp and preparing food as simple as possible. You will be bundled up, cold, and fumbling. As soon as you have set up your cooking area, start to melt snow for drinking water. When it's time for dinner, quickly heat a filling meal. (See Home-Dried One-Pot Meals, Chapter 1.)

Winter Camping List

Most gear used for winter camping is the same as that used for summer camping, with the additions of skis or snowshoes, additional warm clothing, extra fuel, and more food. You can rent a four-season tent, a backpack, and skis, boots, poles, or snowshoes. If you don't have a sturdy trowel or a telescoping or folding shovel, buy one. Store it in your vehicle when you aren't snow camping, for digging out your car in emergencies, campfire safety, cat sanitation, and general camp use.

Take items listed in Backpack List, Chapter 2, plus items specific to winter camping adventures as listed below

Borrow, Rent, or Buy Equipment

Skis, poles, boots, snowshoes, portable stove, tent, and backpacks can be borrowed or rented inexpensively. This is a perfect way to

WINTER CAMPING LIST

Skis, Snowshoes, and Accessories

☐ Skis

    ☐ Wax, if required. Waxless skis save weight and time spent waxing and rewaxing skis while on the move.

☐ Poles. Adjustable poles telescope to store compactly. Adjust their length as needed for cross-country skiing, snowshoeing, or hiking.

lightweight snowshoe

telescoping pole

☐ Skins, if needed. Cloth climbing skins attach to the bottoms of your skis. They help prevent sliding while ascending or descending very steep icy slopes.

or

☐ Snowshoes and poles

Repair Kit for Skis

☐ Duct tape, electrical tape, or strapping tape

☐ Epoxy

☐ 4-inch length of PVC tubing, with a diameter slightly larger than your ski poles. (Mend broken ski pole with tape, then slide tubing over tape and apply additional tape over both ends of the tubing.)

☐ Extra ski tip

☐ Extra basket for ski pole

☐ Extra binding screws

178

WINTER CAMPING LIST (CONTINUED)

☐ Screwdriver, appropriate size

☐ Wire

Shelter

☐ 4-season sleeping bag or 3-season bag with liner

☐ 4-season tent that can withstand heavy snow and wind

☐ 1-inch-thick closed-cell foam, or 2-inch-thick open-cell foam, sleeping pad

☐ Grommeted tarp. Use as a windbreak or as a roof in your kitchen area.

☐ Folding or telescoping shovel, or sturdy hand trowel, for digging snow cave, constructing windbreaks and work areas, and keeping tent free of snow during storms.

☐ Perforated snow stakes for tent instead of smooth stakes

Clothing

☐ Ski boots, or use hiking boots with snowshoes, or with skis equipped with cable bindings

☐ Athletic shoes, or down-filled booties and waterproof overboots, to wear in camp

☐ Liner gloves and heavy, waterproof mittens or gloves

☐ Waterproof and windproof jacket

☐ Waterproof and windproof pants

☐ Balaclava

☐ Wool or nylon trousers

☐ Wool or synthetic long underwear

☐ Down or fleece vest

Safety Supplies

☐ Altimeter to aid in map-reading when vision is obscured by bad weather

☐ Extra plastic bags. Use as

WINTER CAMPING LIST (CONTINUED)

emergency mittens or gaiters, or as vapor barriers worn between liner socks and heavy outer socks.

☐ Emergency blanket (space blanket). Use during the day while resting, then place under sleeping pad at night, silver side up, for extra warmth.

☐ Electronic avalanche beacon or avalanche cord

Food and Water

☐ Extra fuel, ½ pint per person per day for melting snow for drinking water

☐ Extra stove and pot for melting snow

☐ Extra closed-cell foam pads for seating and as bases for portable stoves

☐ Several layers of heavy aluminum foil. Place foil between foam pads and portable stoves.

☐ Thermal mug to keep food and drinks hot. In freezing temperatures, metal cups will chill hot food instantly.

☐ Extra high-energy snacks

☐ Extra sponges for drying and cleaning tent and other equipment.

test before you buy. Don't camp in cold weather with less than adequate equipment. You need a tent that can withstand winter storms, a good pair of boots, and a warm sleeping bag.

Winter Camping with Children

If your children are aged three or older and are eager for adventure, try a simple, very low mileage, one-night winter camping trip. If the children become uncomfortable, you can easily return the short distance to your vehicle. Take extra flashlight batteries in case you need to ski or snowshoe out after dark.

Rent cross-country skis or snowshoes for children who are old enough and coordinated enough to be on their own feet (usually about age eight). Younger children can be pulled in a lightweight fiberglass sled. Bundled up in a down jacket or sleeping bag, toddlers can enjoy the ride. When children outgrow the sled, use it to haul your equipment.

Be sure to take a lot of extra warm clothing, especially socks, which can also be used as mittens. Keep children warm, protected against strong sun, and well fed and hydrated.

Kitchen

I do not use my portable stove inside my tent. Perhaps I'm haunted by memories of the ill-fated Scott party in Antarctica. Robert Falcon Scott, leading a British exploration party, reached the South Pole in January 1912, just a month later than Roald Amundsen and his Norwegian team, who were first to arrive and plant their country's flag. (See the Winter Reading List earlier in this chapter for books written by Scott and by Cherry-Garrard, a surviving member of his party.) Scott's team, disappointed and beset by hardship, attempted the return journey from the pole. On the way back, Scott and the members of his party who accompanied him to the pole died from the effects of scurvy, injuries, horrendous blizzards, and their stove's fumes inside their tightly sealed tent.

There are many good reasons to cook away from, not inside, your tent. The danger of fire from a stove flare-up is too great, the lack of ventilation can cause deadly, odorless carbon monoxide poisoning, and, at the least, a spilled pot of boiling soup could burn you and damage your equipment. Instead, rig up a tarp, if needed, to protect your kitchen area from snow, wind, or rain. If the weather is simply too stormy to heat food, see Storm Feasts, this chapter, for ready-to-eat meals. During very cold, windy weather, consider heating your hot meal at noon, then picnicking in your tent with ready-to-eat Storm Feasts during the evening.

Create a comfortable kitchen well away from your tent. Using a shovel or trowel, make a snow block counter for your stove, an extra work counter, a windbreak wall,

snow kitchen

and even seating in the lee of the wall, if desired. If it's very windy, or snowing, construct two or three high walls around the kitchen area and use your tarp as a roof. Pile snow over the edges of the tarp to hold it firmly in place. Let all of your snow constructions sit for half an hour before you use them; this will give the snow time to firm up. Place a small, closed-cell foam pad, covered by several layers of heavy-duty aluminum foil, under your stove. The pad and foil will keep the snow beneath the stove from melting. Protect your stove's flame with a windscreen. The foam pad and windscreen will keep your stove from losing heat; it will operate more efficiently.

Emphasize dehydrated meals. (See Home-Dried One-Pot Meals, Chapter 1.) These meals need only heating, not cooking, in camp. In winter conditions, you need hot food, but you'll want to spend as little time as possible preparing that hot food. You won't want to stand outside cooking in icy winds and subfreezing temperatures.

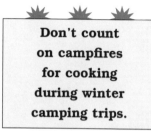

Don't count on campfires for cooking during winter camping trips.

A good-quality portable stove will make your cold weather trip more enjoyable and may save your life. Locating usable fuel for a wood fire may be impossible. Don't count on campfires for cooking during winter camping trips unless you know for certain you'll be able to find burnable wood in your chosen area. Carry a stove that lights easily and burns hot, even in freezing weather. When buying a stove, check the BTUs listed on various stoves. Talk to experienced winter campers. The portable stove you choose for winter camping must be powerful and reliable. Two or more stoves will be needed by a large winter camping party.

Fuel is an important concern while camping in cold weather. Take extra, since you will need it for melting snow for drinking water as well as for cooking. Allow ½ pint of extra fuel per person per day just for melting snow for drinking water. Keep your fuel warm; it will burn more efficiently. Bundle fuel containers in plastic bags and keep them inside your sleeping bag at night. Use caution if you must refill your stove with fuel. In subzero temperatures, gasoline or kerosene spilled on bare skin can cause frostbite.

Extra Calories

Plan to eat well. You will be hungrier while winter camping than you have ever been in your life. A skier carrying a backpack in cold temperatures can burn more

You will be hungrier while winter camping than you have ever been in your life.

than 5,000 calories a day—far more than during normal activities at home. Plan to eat six times a day: breakfast, snack, lunch, snack, dinner, and a final, important, evening snack that will keep you warm through the night. Don't skimp on concentrated fats and sugars. Include a generous selection of the following foods:

Fats

- Butter or margarine (Store this in a wide-mouthed screw-top or snap-top plastic container. These are invaluable energy sources. Spread on crackers or bread and add to hot foods.)
- Beef jerky
- Dry salami
- Canned meat
- Sardines in oil
- Nuts
- Nut butter (Store in a wide-mouthed screw-top or snap-top plastic container.)
- High-fat cheese, such as cheddar

Sugars

candy

- Pound cake
- Candy, such as caramels and butterscotch
- Dried fruit
- Fudge
- Chocolate (Eat other candy during the day for quick energy. Chocolate, which is digested more slowly than other candies, is best eaten during the evening.)
- Hot cocoa (See Instant Cocoa recipe in Chapter 4.)

Storm Feasts

Select some favorite foods that can be enjoyed in your tent without cooking. Label them "storm feasts" and save them for times when you must wait out blizzards or cold rainstorms in your tent.

- Crackers (See Storing Food in Chapter 1 for a suggestion on how to store fragile food.)
- Chapatis
- Pita bread
- Boston brown bread
- Beef jerky
- Dry salami
- Aged hard cheese, such as Parmesan, Romano, or dry Monterey Jack (See Storing Food, Chapter 1, for cheese-preserving tips.)
- Canned meat or meat substitute
- Canned fish
- Smoked fish
- Dried fruit slices or fruit leather
- Gourmet chocolate
- Cookies and bars
- Hard candy
- Granola mixed with dry milk and dried fruit, just add water
- Butter or margarine, honey, and jam (Store in wide-mouthed screw-top or snap-top plastic containers.)

Chop fresh spinach.

You'll be glad you packed some home-dried one-pot meals that heat quickly when you are cold and hungry. Try this spicy seafood dish.

Maryland Crab Casserole

4 servings

1. Preheat oven to 375° F. Oil a 9 by 13-inch glass casserole dish.

2. Mix together in a large bowl:

   1 bunch fresh spinach, washed, drained, and chopped

   2 pounds crabmeat, or imitation crab, shredded

   1 cup grated cheddar cheese

   1 cup nonfat milk

   1 cup cracker or bread crumbs

   Juice of 1 fresh lemon

   2 teaspoons dry mustard

   2 teaspoons Worcestershire sauce

   ¼ cup chopped green onions

   ¼ cup chopped fresh parsley

   ¼ teaspoon cayenne pepper

   ¼ teaspoon sea salt

3. Spread mixture in casserole dish and bake for 30 minutes, or until browned.

4. See Home-Dried One-Pot Meals, Chapter 1, for dehydrating instructions.

5. Spread on plastic-covered dehydrator trays and dehydrate for 4½ hours at 145° F.

6. To rehydrate, cover with water, boil, stir, and serve.

Spanish Tomato Soup

4 servings

This is a very warming soup.

1. Heat a Dutch oven or large skillet over medium heat. Add:

   2 tablespoons olive oil

   When the oil is hot, add and cook, stirring, until soft:

   2 onions, finely chopped

2. Add:

   2 cups any variety stock

   3½ cups chopped tomatoes, fresh or canned

   4 tablespoons fresh mint, chopped, or 2 tablespoons dried, crumbled

   1 clove garlic, minced

   1 teaspoon honey

   2 teaspoons hot sauce

   ½ teaspoon sea salt

   Bring to a boil, then reduce heat to low, cover, and simmer for 30 minutes.

3. Remove from heat and stir in:

   ⅓ cup dry sherry

4. Let cool slightly. Whirl in blender until smooth.

5. See Home-Dried One-Pot Meals, Chapter 1, for dehydrating instructions.

6. Pour the soup onto plastic-covered dehydrator trays and dehydrate for 5½ hours at 145° F.

7. To rehydrate, cover with water, boil, stir, and serve with Crispy Crackers (see Chapter 7) or Peanut Chapatis (see Chapter 2).

Sweet and Sour Jerky

Makes 1 cup beef jerky pieces

It's easy and inexpensive to make your own delicious beef jerky at home.

1. Place in freezer until partially frozen:

   1 pound lean steak, flank or round

2. Remove and discard fat.

3. Slice the meat into ¼-inch-thick strips.

4. Mix together in a glass casserole dish:

   1 tablespoon tamari soy sauce

   1 tablespoon vinegar

   2 tablespoons grapefruit juice

   2 tablespoons packed brown sugar

   ½ teaspoon Liquid Smoke

   2 cloves garlic, minced

   Hot sauce to taste

5. Marinate the beef strips in the sauce, stirring to coat, for 3 minutes.

6. See Home-Dried One-Pot Meals (Chapter 1) for dehydrating instructions.

7. Place the beef strips directly on lightly oiled dehydrator trays and dehydrate for 6 hours at 145° F.

Toffee Bars

Makes 24 bars

These ready-to-eat bars are filling and provide needed sugar.

1. Preheat oven to 350° F. Oil a 9 by 13-inch baking pan.

2. Mix together in a medium bowl:

   2 cups packed brown sugar

   1 cup unbleached white flour

   1 cup whole wheat flour

3. Stir in:

   $\frac{1}{3}$ cup corn oil

4. Beat together in a large bowl:

   $\frac{1}{2}$ cup nonfat milk

   2 whole eggs plus 2 egg whites

   1 teaspoon baking powder

   2 teaspoons vanilla extract

5. Set aside 1 cup of the flour mixture to be used as filling. Add the rest of the flour mixture to the milk mixture. Beat the batter well. Spread half of the batter in the oiled pan.

6. Sprinkle the reserved cup of flour mixture evenly over the batter. Sprinkle over the top of the flour mixture:

   10 ounces English toffee bits or 12 ounces semisweet chocolate chips

   $\frac{1}{2}$ cup chopped pecans or walnuts

   $\frac{1}{4}$ cup toasted wheat germ

7. Pour the remaining batter over the filling. Bake for 35 minutes, or until a toothpick inserted in center comes out clean.

8. Cool completely. Cut into bars. Wrap bars individually in plastic. (See Storing Foods, Chapter 1.)

Protect Equipment

A tent with a vestibule lets you store all of your equipment underneath the tent's fly, safe from snow or rain. If your backpacks must be left outside, keep them dry. Cover them with large plastic trash bags, well secured with nylon cord. Store them where you will be able to easily find them again, even if several feet of snow accumulate during the night. We once lost supplies stored outside the tent during a heavy storm; the snow had completely buried what we thought were tall markers.

Keep all of your equipment as dry as possible. Take advantage of sun and wind while you are in camp; air and dry your damp equipment whenever you can.

Protect fresh foods, and your water supply, from freezing. Don't store butter, cheese, peanut butter, honey, or jelly in squeeze tubes when temperatures are below freezing. You won't be able to squeeze the food out of frozen tubes. Store these foods in wide-mouthed screw-top or snap-top plastic containers. Wrap your food and keep it as warm as possible in the center of your pack. I like to keep my water bottle inside the sleeping bag, in a plastic bag covered with a cozy sock.

Drinking Water

Your need for drinking water while winter camping is tremendous. You will perspire profusely while on the move, and your body's reservoir of water will evaporate in the intense sun on the snow. Cool winter temperatures disguise dehydration. Take care to drink enough water. (See Avoid Dehydration and Heatstroke, Chapter 1.)

Always try to camp near unfrozen, running water. A ready source of running water will save you the tedious, time-consuming chore of melting snow for your drinking water. To collect water from a stream, fasten a collapsible bucket to the end of a ski pole. Use it to scoop water from otherwise unreachable water sources. Use great caution on or near open water. When you are gathering water, have a companion stand nearby who can haul you out with an outstretched ski pole if you slip into a creek or break through ice-covered water.

Sometimes winter camps are unavoidably located far from running water. If so, you must allow plenty of time to turn ice or snow into drinking water. As soon as you stop for the day, set up your stove area and begin to melt snow for drinking water. Gather a lot of ice, or the wettest, iciest snow you can find. Dry, fluffy snow contains more air than water; it takes a great deal of dry snow to create a pot of drinking water. Pile your supply of ice or icy snow near your stove. First place at least an inch of reserved "starter" water in your cooking pot. This will help start the snow melting and prevent the hot stove from scorching your pot. Then add wet ice or snow, a little at a time, and heat until melted. Stand by to prevent scorching, and add more ice when needed. Late in the day, prepare adequate amounts of water for drinking overnight and fixing breakfast. You won't want to perform this task in the morning when it's usually even colder than during the evening. Store canteens of warm water overnight, placed inside plastic bags,

Scoop water from a creek.

then inside socks, at the foot of your sleeping bag. The warm water will help keep you comfortable at night.

If you are spending two or more days in a base camp, set up several water collection systems. These simple methods will turn snow into water while you are ski touring or snowshoeing. Set pots or other containers underneath dripping snowbanks. If you are camped in an all-day full-sun location, set up additional water collectors. Spread large black plastic trash bags or clean, waterproof tarps on the snow. Press depressions into the centers of the bags or tarps, then spread a layer of snow

> Late in the day, prepare adequate amounts of water for drinking overnight and fixing breakfast.

over each of them. The snow will quickly melt and fill the depressions. If the days are quite warm and sunny, make some larger water collectors. Fill several large black plastic bags with snow, then close the tops of the bags securely. The snow will melt during the day. At the end of the day, pour the collected water into jugs or canteens. Store the water inside your tent overnight, preferably next to or inside your sleeping bag. Water left outside will surely refreeze.

Winter Tent

When you spend the night outdoors in snow country, your tent must be sturdy enough to withstand heavy snow and high winds. A four-season tent is made of a thicker and slightly heavier fabric than a three-season tent. It is very sturdy, with double- and triple-stitched seams. Most important, its shape is designed to deflect snow and wind. To accommodate two campers and all of their winter equipment, select a tent, preferably with a vestibule, that sleeps two to three people. A tall, pyramidal tent, well staked against the wind, is best in heavy, wet snowstorms. The walls of a pyramidal

tent are so steep, snow slides right off. Dome tents are roomiest and
deflect wind very well, but snow can build up on some dome tents.

A heavy, wet snowstorm can collapse a tent and bend, or even
break, the tent poles. If your tent is damaged, you will be in trouble. During a blizzard, snow can pile up unbelievably fast; stay alert.
Keep your tent clear of snow. To remove light amounts of snow,
gently hit the tent from the inside. During heavy storms, you may
wake up and find that the interior of your tent seems greatly
reduced in size. Snow has piled up against
the tent, and the walls and ceiling are
pressing toward you. Go outside and gently sweep the snow off the tent with your
waterproof gloves or mittens, then shovel the snow away from the tent's base. Be
careful not to damage your tent with the
shovel. Pile the snow well away from the
tent. You may need to clear the tent of snow several times during
a blizzard. It is hard to crawl out of your sleeping bag at 2 A.M. and
go out into the storm, but well worth it to keep yourself and your
tent from being engulfed by snow.

> **Before your
> winter camping trip,
> try setting up your
> tent while wearing
> your gloves.**

When selecting a tent, choose one that can be set up easily, then practice assembling it at home. Before your winter
camping trip, try setting up your tent while wearing your
gloves. You won't want to handle freezing cold aluminum
poles and stakes with your bare hands. It's slightly cum-
bersome, but you'll find you can set up your tent while
gloved, especially if you are wearing only your thin
liner gloves. Do everything you can beforehand to
make tent setup faster and easier. For example, put
large, easy-to-grasp pulls on all zippers. Lubricate
the zippers. Thin, straight tent stakes are
designed for use in soil. In ice and snow, use
perforated snow stakes, or create blocks of snow
and tie the tent's lines to the blocks.

**perforated snow
stake for a tent**

Sleep Warm

We have lightweight down liner bags that fit inside our regular-weight down sleeping bags, converting our three-season bags to four-season bags. The liners make excellent summer bags on their own; we also use them while traveling abroad in summer and, fully unzipped and opened flat, as comforters at home.

For winter camping you will need a sleeping bag with about a zero-degree Fahrenheit rating. Borrow, rent, or buy a four-season bag or a liner that you can use in tandem with your three-season bag. Don't try to camp on snow with a less than adequate sleeping bag. Check the temperature ratings when you buy or rent a sleeping bag. If you normally tend to feel cold while sleeping, choose a bag rated for even colder temperatures. A sleeping bag that draws up snugly around your face is essential for winter camping. Since you may want to keep your boots, water bottle, and a fuel bottle inside your sleeping bag at night during very cold weather, a bag with about a foot of extra length is a real advantage.

Protect your goose-down sleeping bag from the moisture exuded by your body during the night. In cold winter weather, this moisture often accumulates as frost or water droplets on the inside walls of the tent. Keep your bag away from the tent's walls. Wipe the walls with a sponge. Keep the tent as dry as possible. Maintain some cross ventilation in your tent. Even when it's very cold, leave both doors, or the door and the window, partially open. A down sleeping bag covered with nonbreathable material, such as a waterproof bivouac sack or a foil emergency blanket, will get damp overnight. While you are sleeping, moisture from your body accumulates between the sleeping bag and the bivouac sack. Let your bag breathe, especially if it is filled with down. A synthetic bag, while not as warm or compact as down, does hold warmth even when damp.

A thoroughly soaked down-filled sleeping bag is useless. If you frequently camp in very damp winter conditions, a synthetic-filled sleeping bag may be a wise choice, even though it is not as warm as goose down and is heavier and bulkier.

When you are lying in your tent, protect your body from cold coming up from the ground. Be sure your sleeping pad is adequately thick for cold weather: about two inches for an open-cell foam pad, about one inch for a closed-cell foam pad. In winter, air mattresses feel cold; you may be more comfortable sleeping on a foam pad. For extra warmth, spread an emergency blanket (space blanket) underneath your sleeping pad, with the shiny silver side of the blanket facing up. Pad your body with your extra clothes. Fold the clothes, then place them either between the sleeping bag and the sleeping pad or inside the sleeping bag. Clothing stored in your pack is wasted insulation. Put your clothing on, or put it underneath you. Place something—anything—underneath you if you feel cold at night. Your flattened, empty backpack placed under your sleeping pad will keep you several inches away from the cold ground. If you still can't get warm, wake a companion and ask him or her to get in your sleeping bag with you.

> **If you are caught in a sudden snowstorm, use your trowel, shovel, or even your cooking pot to scoop out an amazingly warm snow cave.**

When camping in very cold weather, get into your sleeping bag early, before the cold evening air chills you down after a day of vigorous exercise. You should feel warm when you first get into your bag. If you're cold, drink a cup of hot cocoa and do some jumping jacks before you go to bed. Wear three or four layers of dry clothing when you first climb into your sleeping bag, including your knit hat and gloves. Slowly remove one layer of clothing at a time as you and your sleeping bag warm up. Place your clothing underneath you in your sleeping bag as you remove it.

Take Your Boots to Bed

After a day on snow, ice, and wet, cold ground, your boots will be wet inside and out. Even well-cared-for waterproofed boots will get wet in winter conditions. Without adequate care overnight, they will be frozen and contorted in the morning. Frozen boots are painful, if not impossible, to put on your feet. Bag your boots, gaiters, and mittens in one or more heavy plastic bags and put them inside the foot of your sleeping bag when you get into the bag at night. It will take a little longer for you to feel warm inside the bag, but you will be rewarded with warm, comfortable boots in the morning. Keep damp socks in your sleeping bag. Your body heat will warm and dry them overnight.

Warm and dry your boots overnight.

Sponges

Keep several large sponges inside the tent at all times. During a storm, fine snow drifts through the tiny cracks of even the best tent. Sponges mop up puddles, wipe condensation from the tent's walls, clean up spills, and remove mud and snow from boots before you bring them into your tent.

sponge

Digging In

Carry a sturdy, lightweight digging tool—a folding or telescoping shovel or a sturdy trowel—with you at all times. If you are caught in a sudden snowstorm, use your trowel, shovel, or even your cooking pot to scoop out an amazingly warm snow cave. Tunnel into deep snow on the side of a hill, or a large tree well. If you are in open country, first create a large pile of snow, then tunnel into it. Face your tunnel's entrance away from the wind. Be sure to wear waterproof clothing while digging, and be careful not to become overheated and soaked with perspiration. Dig upward into the hill, tree well, or pile of snow, throwing the snow downhill, until you have enough space to crawl inside.

Human Waste Disposal

In deep snow, urinate well away from camp and trail. Kick snow over urine to hide it. Pack out your feces. After defecating on the snow, place a thin plastic bag over your hand like a mitten; pick up your feces, turn the bag inside out, and secure the top of the bag. Deposit the feces in the thin plastic bag inside a heavy, opaque zip-top plastic bag. Strap this bag to the outside of your pack; in winter conditions, it will freeze and create no odor problem. If you are in a very remote location, dig a hole in the snow—as deep as possible—and cover the feces with snow. Be careful to stay away from watercourses, and remember that your feces will be exposed when the snow melts. Pack out or burn all toilet paper. Keep a pack of matches handy; store some in the plastic bag that holds your toilet paper.

7

INTERNATIONAL CAMPING

We pitched our small backpack tent on an empty Scottish beach near a remote village. A little boy watched us in amazement. Later he walked by with his father and whispered, "Dad, a mon and a lady come walkin' down the road. They set up that little tiny tent, and then they crawlt into it!"

*   *   *

When traveling abroad, the less you spend, the richer your experience. If you camp during your next international vacation, your world view will change. Your trip will be intimate and filled with surprises. Since most North American travelers isolate themselves in hotels, as a camper you will encounter a colorful array of local people and interesting tourists from other countries.

Not only is international camping economical, it's truly an adventure. As with backpacking at home, you are independent. The basics are in your pack. You can eat and sleep anywhere you'd like. Many of the world's lodgings, indoors or out, don't provide the extra amenities that we accept as the norm. You will often need your own soap, towel, and cup while staying in a very basic hotel or private rented room, as well as in a hostel or a campground. When you travel as a camper, you're ready for anything.

Backpackers are respected. After all, you are taking time to see the sights close up . . . and taking time to meet people. Campers care enough to have a real look at the country's culture, not just rush through the major tourist attractions. As a camper, you will be a roving ambassador of goodwill. If you conduct yourself as an ambassador, you will be treated as one.

> **When traveling abroad, the less you spend, the richer your experience.**

Camping Choices

While planning your trip, study current guidebooks, national tourist board information, and the Internet to determine camping feasibility at your destination. Are the country's campgrounds and national and regional parks mentioned favorably? Does your chosen area offer camping? Can you camp conveniently close to the attractions you want to visit? What will it cost to camp at public and private campgrounds or in national parks? Camping is an excellent alternative to expensive lodgings in high-priced regions such as northern Europe.

The Lonely Planet or Berkeley Guides series of budget guidebooks detail the types of camping that are available and what sort of weather is likely during the time of your visit. This information will help you determine your choice of equipment. Backcountry camping during many nights of your trip, or sleeping outdoors in cold or wet weather, requires a tent, a three-season sleeping bag, and a sleeping pad. Stays in hostels and very basic informal camping in hot

> **You will often need your own soap, towel, and cup while staying in a very basic hotel or private rented room as well as in a hotel or a campground.**

climates may require only a sheet-sack, a very lightweight sleeping bag, or a combination of the two.

Each country has its own camping style. In Eastern Europe, campgrounds feature cozy, old-fashioned bungalows with tiny kitchens. French campers set vases of colorful wildflowers outside their tents. Some countries provide huts, with meals, especially in their national parks. Study the guidebooks to learn what is available. Plan ahead and reserve hut spaces in popular areas. Campgrounds in some countries rent both tents and sleeping bags to tourists. Plan carefully before you pack your equipment.

> **Some countries provide huts, with meals, especially in their national parks.**

Backpacking in a national park anywhere in the world is an unforgettable experience and could well be made the centerpiece of your international camping trip. Whether you sleep in the park's campgrounds or cross the remote interior of the park carrying a backpack, you can walk the trails and enjoy the views, history, wildlife, and encounters with interesting people.

Typical public and private campgrounds outside North America provide only a small space for a vehicle and a tent—no picnic table or cooking grill. Coin-operated hot showers are the norm. These are not the large, heavily forested campsites found throughout North America. Although they tend to be clean, safe, and quiet, international campgrounds can be a bit utilitarian. They do provide a shower and an inexpensive place to sleep near the sights you want to visit. Best of all, international campgrounds give you an opportunity to meet interesting campers from all over the world.

> **Campgrounds in some countries rent both tents and sleeping bags to tourists.**

If camping sounds like a good choice at your destination, plan to spend about half your nights camping. You could, for example, sleep outdoors whenever the weather is good and you are visiting national parks, rural areas, or small cities, then sleep indoors in hostels, hotels, or bed and breakfast lodgings while touring large cities or during inclement weather. If your plans include

> **Coin-operated hot showers are the norm.**

camping for less than half of your vacation, you may not want to carry your sleeping bag, sleeping pad, and tent. If you carry them, use them—and enjoy your special adventure.

path along the River Emajog, Estonia

Informal Camping

Outside the organized campgrounds, you can often backpack in national and regional parks and can sometimes camp informally in rural fields, mountain areas, and on beaches.

Always ask if, and where, you can camp. Talk to park personnel, tourist boards, local residents, and other travelers. If you see nearby dwellings while hiking in a rural area, knock on the door of the nearest house. Ask if you can set up your tent in their field. If they cannot accommodate you themselves, you'll likely be given a lead to another camp spot. Always explain that you will not be cooking or lighting any fires. Avoid lighting stoves or campfires when camping informally on either public or private property. Picnic on cold food instead. Keep a neat, courteous, low profile.

Pyrénées National Park, France

Private or Public Transportation

Rented vehicles will let you camp in style in campgrounds, on beaches, and in national parks. If you rent a fully equipped camping vehicle, you can even leave your tent at home. With small children in your party, this could be your best camping choice.

Hiking, traveling on trains and local buses when necessary, and camping informally and at campgrounds is an adventure. We have met many helpful local residents who offered us rides to remote campgrounds, pointed out informal campsites, or even invited us to sleep on their property. Once a local bus driver detoured miles off his route to deliver us to a rural campground's gates.

> **If you have small children in your party, renting a fully equipped camping vehicle could be your best camping choice.**

Water Purification

Never drink untreated water. In most countries, safe bottled water is available everywhere. You will need to either carry purchased bottled water, carry and use a portable microporous water filter, use iodine tablets, or boil all your water for three minutes. In some parts of the world waterborne viruses are prevalent. While traveling in these areas, you'll need to peel all of your fruits and vegetables, and you may need to add iodine tablets to the water you have pumped through your microporous filter. Check with your local public health department before your trip, and follow their cautionary advice. A serious bout with waterborne illness could ruin your camping trip, and symptoms could linger for months after you return home.

Check with your local public health department or with the Centers for Disease Control and Prevention (CDC) before your trip, and follow their cautionary advice. Telephone the CDC's International Travelers' Hotline: (404) 332-4559, or check their current warnings about your destination's food, insect, and water-borne diseases on the Internet: www.cdc.gov.

Food

Keep international camp cookery simple. Take only a lightweight portable stove, a small aluminum pot, and one Sierra cup and aluminum spoon per person. Firewood may not be available; rely on a portable stove. Your portable stove must be an international model that can be converted to burn kerosene. Kerosene is the fuel

view of Brothers Water, Lake District National Park, England

that is most widely available everywhere in the world except North America, where white gas is the most frequently used fuel. *Fuel is not allowed on any aircraft.* You must drain your stove and buy fuel abroad. Do not bring your North American propane stove; the fittings of foreign "camping gaz" stoves are different than our propane stoves. Here are your two best choices:

> **Kerosene is the fuel that is the most widely available everywhere in the world except North America, where white gas is the most frequently used fuel.**

- Take an international convertible gas stove that will burn kerosene and buy fuel abroad, or
- Buy a kerosene or propane stove and fuel after you have arrived at your destination. Reuse it on other international camping trips.

One-pot home-dried meals (see Chapter 1) will get you started on your international trip. Supplement your diet with instant dried soups and canned foods; they are ubiquitous worldwide and are quick to heat. Add some fresh local breads and fruit, and stop at delicatessens for prepared salads and other treats.

Begin your adventure with the following recipes.

Jamaican Chicken

4 servings

1. Heat a heavy Dutch oven over medium heat. Add:
   2 tablespoons olive oil
2. When the oil is hot, add and cook, stirring, for 10 minutes, or until lightly browned:
   1 onion, minced

4 large russet potatoes, scrubbed but not peeled, finely
chopped

3. Add and cook 10 minutes longer:
   3 boneless, skinless chicken breast halves, sliced into
   small, thin strips
   1 green bell pepper, finely chopped
   3 cloves garlic, minced
   2 teaspoons chili powder
   2 teaspoons curry powder
   2 teaspoons minced fresh thyme, or 1 teaspoon dried

4. Add and bring to a boil:
   2 cups chopped tomatoes, fresh or canned
   2 tablespoons tamari soy sauce

5. Reduce heat and simmer for 20 minutes, stirring occasionally.

6. See Home-Dried One-Pot Meals, Chapter 1, for
   dehydrating instructions.

7. Spread the casserole on plastic-covered dehydrator
   trays and dehydrate for 5½ hours at 145° F.

8. To rehydrate, cover with water, boil, stir, and serve.

Barbecued Tofu

4 servings

1. Heat in a large, heavy skillet over medium heat:
   1 tablespoon canola oil
   When the oil is hot, add and stir:
   1 onion, minced
   When the onion is lightly browned, stir in:
   2 pounds tofu, rinsed and drained, crumbled

½ cup barbecue sauce

½ cup green taco sauce

1 teaspoon chili powder

1 tablespoon honey

2 tablespoons Worcestershire sauce

½ teaspoon Liquid Smoke

2. Simmer for 20 minutes.

3. See Home-Dried One-Pot Meals, Chapter 1, for dehydrating instructions.

4. Spread tofu on plastic-covered dehydrator trays and dehydrate for 5 hours at 145° F.

5. To rehydrate, cover with water, boil, stir, and serve with Peanut Chapatis (see Chapter 2 or Crispy Crackers; recipe on next page).

Cart horse, Trakai,
Lithuania

Crispy Crackers

Makes 10 dozen crackers

**These crackers will stay fresh for weeks.
See Storing Food, Chapter 1.**

1. Preheat oven to 350° F.

2. Lightly oil 2 large baking sheets.

3. Mix together in a large bowl:
   - 1 cup whole wheat flour
   - 1 cup unbleached white flour
   - 3 tablespoons wheat germ
   - 3 teaspoons packed brown sugar
   - 1 teaspoon baking powder
   - ½ teaspoon sea salt

4. Cut in:
   - ½ cup butter or margarine
   - ⅔ cup walnuts, finely chopped

   Blend well, then add:
   - ⅔ cup cold water

5. Knead the dough briefly, then turn it out onto a floured board.

6. Roll dough as thin as possible.

7. Cut the dough into 1 by 2½-inch rectangles; they do not need to be even.

8. Place crackers on oiled baking sheets. Prick them all over with a fork.

9. Bake for 8 to 12 minutes, or until lightly browned on bottoms.

Prick crackers with a fork before baking them.

Picnicking, buying street food, and eating in cafés are alternatives to carrying a stove and cooking pot. You can buy a hot meal at midday in a restaurant when prices are more affordable and then picnic during the evening while camping. Grocery stores and cafés are often located at or near campgrounds, so it's easy to either cook or buy a ready-made supper. We have even received early morning delivery of fresh milk—in glass bottles—directly to our campground tent.

> **You can buy a hot meal at midday in a restaurant when prices are more affordable, then picnic during the evening while camping.**

Air Travel with a Backpack

When you make your flight reservations, ask your travel agent or airline representative what the airline's baggage size and weight limitations are. If the dimensions of your loaded pack are larger than 9 inches by 22 inches by 14 inches, the pack is likely too large to carry onto the aircraft. Your full-sized backpack must be checked in and carried in the plane's luggage compartment.

Before you check in at the baggage counter, plan ahead to protect your pack and its contents. Airport baggage handling equipment can tear off pack straps, crush buckles, and bend metal frames. Don't check your backpack until you have protected it.

Make Your Own Protective Bag

You can sew your own simple rectangular nylon bag. Buy rip-stop nylon fabric and a grommet kit. These are both available from Campmor, a mail-order camping supply; phone 1-800-226-7667 to request a catalog, or see their Web site: www.campmor.com.

Insert grommets around the top of your nylon bag, then slip light metal key rings through the grommets. A small padlock will thread through the key rings. The padlock will hold the bag closed and protect your valuables from pilferage.

Alternatively, purchase a large, lightweight duffel bag. Find a duffel bag with a zipper that can be secured with a small padlock.

Make a protective nylon bag for your backpack.

A large duffel bag is a sturdy choice, and it does have other uses, but it weighs more than a rip-stop nylon bag and doesn't fold up as compactly.

Before checking your baggage, remove your daypack from your backpack. The daypack should contain anything small and important that is not already on your person, such as your camera,

Glendalough, Ireland

lightweight sweater, toothbrush, medications, and guidebook. Keep this daypack with you on the aircraft. Wrap your foam sleeping pad or a pair of trousers and a shirt around your backpack. Do not wrap your sleeping bag around your backpack. Stow your sleeping bag, stove, and other fragile, valuable gear well inside the backpack. Now you're ready to go. Slide the backpack into your nylon bag or duffel. Secure the bag with the small padlock. Add an identification tag at the baggage check-in counter.

Pack Light

Heaving an overstuffed backpack onto an overhead railway luggage rack for the 10th time, you'll wish you hadn't brought your frying pan and heavy sweat suit. Leave home with room to spare in your pack. Take a test walk around your home town; if your loaded pack feels heavy now, it will be unbearable after a few weeks abroad.

Instead of carrying a 16-ounce bottle of shampoo, pack a 1-ounce bottle. You can buy more later. If one of your shirts wears out, you can replace it. We know a well-traveled couple who always wears old clothes when they leave on an international trip. While traveling, they buy clothes that are typical of the country they are visiting. As they accumulate a new wardrobe, they wash their old clothes and give them away.

> When you buy books, souvenirs, and other items of small monetary value, take them to a post office and send them home.

Mail excess materials home. When you buy books, souvenirs, and other items of small monetary value, take them to a post office. The post office will sell you padded envelopes and help you mail your excess baggage home.

When you are touring in cities, don't view the sights while carrying all of your camping equipment. Take advantage of the

> **Secure your full-sized backpack and its contents in a luggage storage locker to enjoy the city in comfort.**

luggage storage lockers at bus and train stations. At the station, take out your daypack, and load it with your camera, jacket, and anything else you'll need while day-touring. Secure your full-sized backpack and its contents in a luggage storage locker. Enjoy the city in comfort.

To keep our packs light, we use ultralight down sleeping bags (they are actually "sleeping bag liners") and an extremely small doghouse-sized tent when camping internationally in warm weather. If we are chilly at night, we wear long underwear and as much of our clothing as we need. A lightweight synthetic knit cap and gloves will help keep you warm all night. An emergency blanket ("space

view of Alsatian vineyards from Vosges Mountains, France

blanket") can be an almost weightless lifesaver. Spread the blanket underneath you, with its edges pulled up loosely at your sides. Most cold comes up from the ground rather than from the air.

If you carry both a lightweight sleeping bag liner and a sheet-sack, you can alternate between sleeping outdoors and hosteling. Choose a *nylon* sheet-sack. These sacks are lightweight and dry quickly. Use the sheet-sack alone or in tandem with your ultralight sleeping bag. This versatile sleeping combination is lighter and more compact than a standard sleeping bag and is warm enough for most summer camping.

A small, lightweight tent will suit most international situations. If you want to travel ultralight, carry only a grommeted tarp and some nylon cord. Keep in mind that you will need trees, walking sticks, or other objects to support your improvised shelter.

Cash Abroad

In industrialized countries worldwide, use your credit card instead of cash. Use it to pay for trains and restaurant meals. Use it wherever it is accepted. When you need cash, automated teller machines (ATMs) are the easiest, least expensive way to obtain a cash advance in the local currency. Your dollars will be converted to the local currency at that day's most favorable rate of exchange. You don't need to wait in line, then struggle through a conversation in another language with a bank teller. You don't need to pay high rates to convert cash or traveler's checks, or carry dangerously large amounts of money. All you need is a bank ATM card or a credit card with a four-digit PIN (Personal Identification Number). Here's how to do it.

> **When you need cash, ATMs are the easiest and least expensive way to obtain a cash advance in the local currency.**

Study guidebooks to determine prices at your destination. Estimate what you'll be spending daily, multiply that figure by the

> Depositing money in your account before the trip precludes extra "cash advance" charges. This will help you avoid interest charges accruing daily on your credit card.

number of days you'll be traveling, then add an extra measure for emergencies. Before you leave home, deposit enough money for your entire trip—plus emergencies—into a bank account or send money, in advance, to your credit card company that is served by international ATMs. Depositing money in your account before the trip precludes extra "cash advance" charges, with interest charges accruing daily on your credit card. ATMs abroad are as easy to use as those at home.

Cawfields Crags, Hadrian's
Wall, England

INTERNATIONAL CAMPING LIST

Whether you are camping for two weeks or for six months, the equipment listed below will keep you comfortable and keep your pack light. This list includes the clothes you will be wearing as well as those you will be carrying. For example, "2 pairs trousers" includes one to wear, and one to pack.

Shelter

- ❏ Backpack, carry-on size, 9 inches by 22 inches by 14 inches or full-sized, with protective sack (see Air Travel with a Backpack, this chapter)
- ❏ Daypack
- ❏ Small, lightweight tent
  - ❏ fly
  - ❏ poles
  - ❏ stakes (including 2 extra)

  or substitute for tent:
  - ❏ grommeted tarp and nylon cord
- ❏ Lightweight sleeping bag and stuff sack (and/or sheet-sack made of cotton, nylon, or silk)
- ❏ Lightweight, compact sleeping pad
- ❏ Ground cloth

Clothing

- ❏ Sturdy walking shoes or lightweight boots
- ❏ 3 pairs heavy socks
- ❏ 3 pairs liner socks
- ❏ Brimmed hat
- ❏ Bandana
- ❏ Silk scarf
- ❏ Waterproof jacket
- ❏ 3 long-sleeved shirts
- ❏ Lightweight, warm, compactible sweater
- ❏ 2 pairs trousers (cotton, wool, or nylon)
- ❏ Nylon belt
- ❏ 3 pairs underpants
- ❏ Synthetic underwear
  - ❏ Bottoms
  - ❏ Long-sleeved top
  - ❏ Short-sleeved top
  - ❏ Knit cap
  - ❏ Lightweight gloves

INTERNATIONAL CAMPING LIST (CONTINUED)

☐ Nylon shorts
☐ Nylon swimsuit

Route Finding

☐ Compass
☐ Maps
☐ Guidebook
☐ Mini travel dictionary and phrase book
☐ Small flashlight and extra batteries

Toiletries

☐ Toilet paper
☐ Comb
☐ Sunscreen
☐ Lip balm with sunscreen
☐ Insect repellent
☐ Shampoo, 1-ounce travel size
☐ Tiny bar of soap in plastic bag
☐ Small synthetic (viscose) towel
☐ Toothbrush

☐ Travel-sized toothpaste
☐ Dental floss
☐ Toothpicks
☐ Razor
☐ Travel-sized shaving cream

First Aid

☐ Bandages
☐ Tweezers
☐ Bismuth tablets
☐ Aspirin
☐ Laxatives
☐ Antibiotics
☐ Antidiarrheal medication
☐ Vitamins
☐ Personal medications

Repair Kit

☐ Needles
☐ Thread
☐ Safety pins
☐ Rubber bands
☐ Rip-stop tape
☐ Tent pole repair sleeve

INTERNATIONAL CAMPING LIST
(CONTINUED)

Foot Kit

- ☐ 2nd Skin
- ☐ Moleskin
- ☐ Rubbing alcohol
- ☐ Tiny blunt-end scissors
- ☐ Micropore tape
- ☐ Needle
- ☐ Nail clippers

Food and Water

- ☐ Water filter or purification tablets
- ☐ Water bottle or canteen
- ☐ *International* portable stove and *empty* fuel container (or buy stove after you have arrived see Food; this chapter)
- ☐ Matches (obtain them after your arrival)
- ☐ Lightweight aluminum pot and lid
- ☐ Sierra cup
- ☐ Lightweight aluminum spoon
- ☐ Folding pocketknife with a corkscrew and can and bottle openers

Tickets and Other Valuables

- ☐ Passport
- ☐ Visa (if required)
- ☐ Air tickets
- ☐ Rail or bus passes
- ☐ Photocopies (reduced size): passport, visa, tickets, passes, credit cards
- ☐ Neck or waistband wallet
- ☐ Leg wallet
- ☐ Cash
- ☐ Credit card
- ☐ Traveler's checks
- ☐ Addresses and phone numbers

Personal

- ☐ Book
- ☐ Camera
- ☐ Extra film
- ☐ Journal
- ☐ Pen and pencil
- ☐ Pocket writing pad

They can be
programmed
for the English
language. When
you can, use an
ATM located out-
side a large bank dur-
ing banking hours.
Check current guidebooks
for availability of ATMs at your
destination. Guidebooks will also
advise you which type of bank ATM
cards and credit cards are most readily accepted at
your destination. Relying on credit cards plus a bit
of cash and some traveler's checks for emergencies
will make your trips smoother. A miniature solar-powered calculator
converts prices quickly.

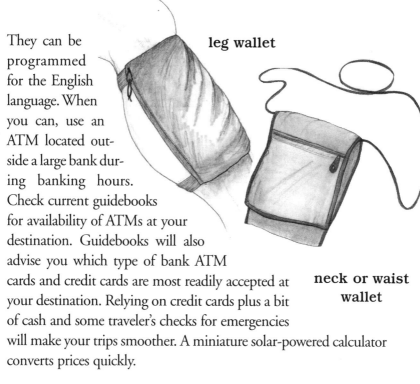

leg wallet

**neck or waist
wallet**

Valuables

Never store hard-to-replace valuables in your backpack. You must
keep your valuables on your body and out of sight. I like to wear
two wallets, both well-secured *underneath* my clothing. In my more
easily accessible neck or waist wallet, I keep passport, passes, tickets, credit and bank cards, phones numbers and addresses, and cash
for the day.

In the leg wallet that is strapped to my calf, I keep the rest of
my monies (some cash, some traveler's checks), air tickets, and
reduced-size photocopies of passport, visa, tickets, passes, and credit cards. In case you lose any of these valuable documents, the photocopies will speed their replacement. The leg wallet is your private
long-term secret storage place. It is so comfortable you will hardly
notice you are wearing it.

In the buttoned pocket of my shirt, I keep a little cash for immediate use, my scratch pad and pencil—for writing out my needs in foreign languages—and a cheat sheet of the most common words and phrases in the native language.

Clothing

Pack very little clothing. Choose colors that won't show stains. Take only sturdy, compact, lightweight pieces that will dry quickly. Test each piece of clothing before your trip. Wear it, then wash it by hand, let it drip dry, and stuff it into a corner of your pack.

Later, take it out and see how it looks. What you see after this experiment is how your clothes will look while you're traveling. Most of the time, you'll be washing your clothing by hand. Look for the following qualities. Will the clothing dry overnight? Is it comfortable? Does it look fairly unrumpled after hand washing, wringing, and packing?

Tailor clothing needs to the region's climate. Study guidebooks to determine temperatures and amount of precipitation during the time of

long-sleeved shirt

your visit. When you travel in cooler climates, very lightweight, unlined wool trousers are comfortable over a wide range of temperatures. Include rain pants for extremely cold, wet regions. In hot climates, very thin cotton, rayon, or nylon trousers—plus shorts—are the best fabric choices. Pack very little clothing, then wear synthetic long underwear under your lightweight shirt and trousers when you feel chilly. The long underwear doubles as warm pajamas.

Long-sleeved, button-front cotton, nylon, or other synthetic shirts with collar, cuffs, button or snap pockets with flaps, and sleeves full enough to be rolled up are comfortable and look good anywhere. Cotton knits such as T-shirts do not dry quickly, are less versatile, and often look too casual when worn in countries outside of North America.

While traveling, wash your shirt, socks, and underwear when weather permits. Wring your wet clothes thoroughly, then dry them as much as possible overnight. If your clothes are still damp in the morning, safety-pin them to the outside of your backpack. They will flap dry as you walk.

view of Levoca, Slovak Republic

Shoes or Boots

Are you planning an ascent of Mt. Blanc? Unless you're engaged in serious mountaineering, or are carrying a heavy pack, very sturdy walking shoes are often the best choice for all-around footwear on international trips. Experiment at home. Wear your loaded pack with boots, then with walking shoes. Choose the footwear that will provide the best balance of comfort and support for your particular trip.

> **Your footwear is your most important piece of equipment.**

If your pack is reasonably light, good walking shoes or very lightweight boots are cooler and more comfortable than backpacking boots. While traveling internationally, you may spend as much time walking on country roads and cobbled city streets as on rocky trails. If your loaded backpack weighs 30 pounds or more, or if you plan a good deal of hiking on rocky trails, wear lightweight, sturdy, waterproofed boots for better support. If your pack is light and you'll be walking on country roads and city streets as often as you will be hiking on trails, wear sturdy, waterproofed walking shoes.

Your footwear is your most important piece of equipment. A blister, even a small one, could ruin your trip. Be sure to pack your foot kit, and take care of potential blisters immediately. (See Be Good to Your Feet, Chapter 1.)

walking shoes

Physical Checkup

Before you leave the country, have a general medical examination. Get any required immunizations. If you need prescribed medications, get your prescriptions filled in advance. Visit your dentist for a checkup.

Journal

Your travel journals will be enjoyed by you and by others in years to come. You don't need to describe every event, every day. Casual overall observations, when you are in the mood, are fun to write, and they make interesting reading later on.

A blank 4 by 6-inch sketchbook makes an excellent journal. Its paper is suitable for both notes and pen-and-ink drawings. I sew three differently colored fabric ribbons to the top of the journal's spine. These markers keep my place for daily writing and drawing in the front section of the journal, in the second section for photo dates and descriptions, and in the third section for expenses. I like to record every expenditure, often with comments that bring the trip alive later on. I can taste that delicate Parisian flan and savor that glass of Belgian Trappist beer again and again. Records help you realistically plan future trips. You will know the

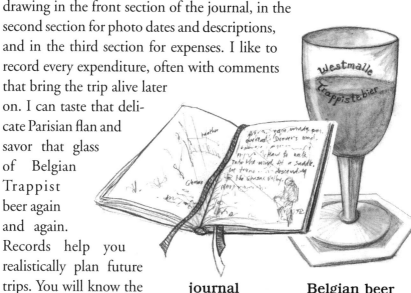

journal   Belgian beer

name, address, phone number, and cost of lodgings, restaurants, and museums—for your future use and as recommendations to your friends. I note if payment was by credit card, so I won't spend more than I have deposited in my account prior to the trip.

Camping with Your International Family

turnpike milestone, Thirsk, England

Imagine seeing a different country from the inside. You are a part of the family, not a tourist, living daily life with your international friends.

Organizations such as International Penfriends, based in Dublin, Ireland, will put you in touch with worldwide correspondents in your age group who share your interests. You can choose countries that appeal to you and select the languages in which you'd like to correspond. Contact International Penfriends in North America through the World Cultural Foundation, P.O. Box 1129, Snoqualmie, WA 98065-1129, telephone (425) 888-7275, fax (425) 888-8500, E-mail: travelr@wcf.org. Make friends through letter writing. Invite your international friends to visit you, and ask if you may visit them.

When you travel complete with camping gear, your friends can more easily accommodate you, even if their house or apartment is tiny. We have camped in friends' gardens and on living room floors, and have enjoyed showing our corner of the world to foreign visitors.

CONCLUSION

It had been a long day on the trail. We ate supper and crawled into our sleeping bags. On this clear, balmy September evening, no tent was needed. As we lay on our backs and gazed at the dark, starry sky, a glow appeared beyond the mountains on the other side of the basin. We held our breath as the round, orange moon rose above the black, jagged peaks, filling the basin with clear light. A marmot scrambled across the sparkling granite boulders. Lichen glowed in the bright-as-day moonlight.

* * *

The beauty and silence experienced on camping trips changes you. Each trip modifies your view, makes you see afresh the gulf between petty pursuits and worthwhile ones. When you return to the world, you carry with you a new perspective from the wilderness. At home, enjoy your luxurious first hot shower, crisp, fresh clothes, and soft bed. Joyfully rejoin your friends, family, and community. Savor the little things you experience every day, fondly recall your most recent bright camping moments, and ponder life's important questions, such as: when can we go camping again? Nature's free show runs continuously. You simply need to go outdoors and experience it.

CAMPING RESOURCES IN THE UNITED STATES AND CANADA

Food Dehydrators

As you prepare for your next camping trip, these dehydrators make it almost impossible to overdry or otherwise ruin your home-dried meals.

Excalibur Products
6083 Power Inn Road
Sacramento, CA 95824
(800) 875-4254

Nesco American Harvest
4064 Peavey Road
Chaska, MN 55318
(800) 288-4545

Maps

Purchase topographic maps prior to your trip. Topo maps are sold at camping, mining, and survey stores. You can also order your U.S. maps from the United States Department of the Interior Geological Survey.

(800) HELP-MAP
FAX: (303) 202-4693
WEB: http://www-nmd.usgs.gov/

Canadian maps and river guides are available from Dog Ears.

Dog Ears
900 Greenbank Road
Suite 327
Ottawa, Ontario, K2J4P6
Canada
E-MAIL: staff@dogears.com
WEB: www.dogears.com/dog-ears.htm

Also request the map symbol index when you order your topo map(s). They are willing to call you back to save you phone charges.

National Park and Campground Information

Bureau of Land Management (BLM) Campgrounds
WEB: www.blm.gov

United States Forest Service Campgrounds
WEB: www.fs.fed.us

National Recreation Reservation Center
(800) 280-CAMP

United States National Park Service
WEB: www.nps.gov

To reserve a National Park Service campsite
(800) 365-2267

Canadian National Parks

Great Outdoor Recreation Pages are on the Web at www.gorp.com. Look in the Canadian Resources section.

State and Provincial Park Information

United States
WEB: camping.guide@miningco.com

Canada
WEB: www.gorp.com

Look in the Canada by Province section.

Ideas for trail hiking and camping in both provincial parks and private campgrounds.

Other Useful Contacts Mentioned in the Book

Outdoor Wilderness Fabrics Inc.
16415 Midland Boulevard
Nampa, ID 83687
(800) OWF-SHOP or (208) 466-1602
FAX: (208) 463-4622
They offer pack cloth, canvas, nylon, fleece, and other outdoor fabrics, patterns, and sewing accessories by mail.

Centers for Disease Control and Prevention
International Travelers' Hotline: (404) 332-4559
WEB: www.cdc.gov

Call to check for current warnings about food, insect, and water-borne diseases at your destination.

International Penfriends
World Cultural Foundation
International Penfriends in North America
P.O. Box 1129
Snoqualmie, WA 98065-1129
(425) 888-7275
FAX: (425) 888-8500
E-MAIL: travelr@wcf.org

An organization that will put you in touch with worldwide correspondents in your age group who share your interests. You can choose countries that appeal to you and select the languages in which you'd like to correspond.

BIBLIOGRAPHY

Davidson, James W., and John Rugge. *The Complete Wilderness Paddler*. New York: Random House, 1983.

Fletcher, Colin. *The Complete Walker III*. New York: Alfred A. Knopf, 1984.

Ganci, Dave. *Desert Hiking*. 3rd ed. Berkeley, CA: Wilderness Press, 1993.

Greenspan, Rick, and Hal Kahn. *The Camper's Companion*. 3rd ed. San Francisco, CA: Foghorn Press, 1996.

Gullion, Laurie. *Canoeing*. Champaign, IL: Human Kinetics Publishers, 1994.

Harmon, Will. *Wild Country Companion*. Helena, MT: Falcon Press Publishing Co., Inc., 1994.

Howe, Steve, et al. *Making Camp*. Seattle, WA: The Mountaineers, 1997.

Jacobson, Cliff. *Camping Secrets*. Merrillville, IN: ICS Books, Inc., 1987.

Juranek, Dennis D., Chief, Epidemiology Activity, Parasitic Diseases Branch, Division of Parasitic Diseases, Centers for Disease Control and Prevention. "Giardiasis." Centers for Disease Control, 1990.

Kuhne, Cecil. *Inflatable Kayaking.* Mechanicsburg, PA: Stackpole Books, 1997.

Maclean, Norman. "USFS 1919: The Ranger, the Cook, and a Hole in the Sky." In *A River Runs Through It and Other Stories.* Chicago: University of Chicago Press, 1976.

Mason, Bill. *Song of the Paddle.* Toronto: Key Porter Books, 1995.

McGinnis, Christopher J. *202 Tips Even the Best Business Travelers May Not Know.* Burr Ridge, IL: Irwin Professional Publishing, 1994.

McManners, Hugh. *The Backpacker's Handbook.* New York: Dorling Kindersley Publishing, Inc., 1995.

Mouland, Michael. *The Complete Idiot's Guide to Hiking, Camping, and the Great Outdoors.* New York: Alpha Books, 1996.

Randall, Glenn. *The Modern Backpacker's Handbook.* New York: Lyons & Burford, 1994.

Ross, Cindy and Todd Gladfelter. *Kids in the Wild.* Seattle, WA: The Mountaineers, 1995.

Rutter, Michael. *Camping Made Easy.* Old Saybrook, CT: The Globe Pequot Press, 1997.

Seidman, David. *The Essential Wilderness Navigator.* Camden, ME: Ragged Mountain Press, 1995.

Steves, Rick. *Europe Through the Back Door.* Santa Fe, NM: John Muir Publications, 1998.

Watters, Ron. *Ski Camping: A Guide to the Delights of Backcountry Skiing.* Rev. ed. Pocatello, Idaho: Great Rift Press, 1989.

Whitman, John. *The Best European Travel Tips.* New York: HarperCollins Publishers, Inc., 1995.

INDEX

ABOUT THE AUTHOR

Linda Frederick Yaffe, who has more than 40 years of camping experience, is also a distance runner, weight trainer, and terrific cook. She is the author of *High Trail Cookery: All-Natural, Home-Dried, Palate-Pleasing Meals for the Backpacker*, Revised Edition, also published by Chicago Review Press. She lives in Auburn, California.